From invites
to overnights
and everything
in between

Best
Party Book
ever!

OCT 2 7 2014

From the Editors of Faithgirlz! and *Girls' Life* magazine

Other books in the growing Faithgirlz!™ library

NONFICTION

Big Book of Quizzes
Fun, Quirky Questions for You and Your Friends
From the editors of Faithgirlz!

Faithgirlz! Handbook
Faithgirlz! Journal
Food, Faith & Fun: A Faithgirlz! Cookbook

Girl Politics
Everybody Tells Me to be Myself but I Don't Know Who I Am
You! A Christian Girl's Guide to Growing Up

DEVOTIONALS
Finding God In Tough Times
No Boys Allowed
What's a Girl to Do?
Girlz Rock
Chick Chat
Real Girls of the Bible
My Beautiful Daughter
Whatever!

BIBLES
NIV Faithgirlz! Bible
NIV Faithgirlz! Backpack Bible

BIBLE STUDIES
Secret Power of Love
Secret Power of Joy
Secret Power of Goodness
Secret Power of Grace

FICTION

The Samantha Sanderson Series
Samantha Sanderson at the Movies (Book One)
Samantha Sanderson on the Scene (Book Two)

The Good News Shoes
Riley Mae and the Rock Shocker Trek (Book One)
Riley Mae and the Ready Eddy Rapids (Book Two)
Riley Mae and the Sole Fire Safari (Book Three)

From Sadie's Sketchbook
Shades of Truth (Book One)
Flickering Hope (Book Two)
Waves of Light (Book Three)
Brilliant Hues (Book Four)

The Girls of Harbor View
Girl Power
Take Charge
Raising Faith
Secret Admirer

Boarding School Mysteries
Vanished (Book One)
Betrayed (Book Two)
Burned (Book Three)
Poisoned (Book Four)

Check out www.faithgirlz.com

ZONDERKIDZ

Best Party Book Ever!
Copyright © 2014 Red Engine, LLC

Requests for information should be addressed to:

Zonderkidz, 3900 Sparks Dr., Grand Rapids, Michigan 49546

ISBN 978-0-310-74600-3

430 2937

Done in association with Red Engine, LLC, Baltimore, MD.

Zonderkidz is a trademark of Zondervan.

Editors: Kim Childress and Karen Bokram
Contributor: Katie Abbondanza
Cover and interior design: Chun Kim
Photography: Lindsay Hite
Writing and styling: Jessica D'Argenio Waller

Printed in China

14 15 16 17 18 /DSC/ 22 21 20 19 18 17 16 15 14 13 12 11 10 9 8 7 6 5 4 3 2 1

TABLE OF CONTENTS

TABLE OF CONTENTS

We think that every day should be a celebration. Whether you're throwing a big birthday bash or just having a dance party by yourself in your bedroom, there are a million little reasons to celebrate this beautiful life. Your task? Getting the soirée started!

We hope this book helps you not only to throw a memorable and creative bash, but also to form new traditions with family and friends, to be a sweet and gracious hostess and ultimately to learn how to make every day even more amazing than the last.

Slip on your party shoes and let's celebrate!

— *the editors*

HOSTESS HINTS

We're serving up expert tips and tricks to make sure you're on top of your game before you even seal and stamp the first invitation.

The surefire way to make your soirée stand out? It's all about the DIY (do it yourself). Those tiny, unique-to-you touches are what your guests will be chatting about long after they go home—and will officially land you the party queen crown. Putting a little effort into the planning and prep of your party means you and your guests will have that much more of a blast. And is there any better reward than that?

HOSTESS HOW-TO

The most important part of any celebration? Making sure you and your guests have an amazing night. The key is that the bash comes off without a hitch through preliminary planning. Psst: Even party planning pros use a handy checklist to help them stay organized. Carve one out a couple days ahead so you can be sure you're stocked up on things like plates, cups and napkins, and whatever snacks and drinks you'll be buying or making. The day before, make a list of all the things that need to be done before people arrive, like cleaning the house and hanging up any decorations. The day of, cross off any last-minute items, like arranging the furniture and setting the food table. Want extra brownie points? Offer to vacuum the living room for Mom or help Dad tidy up the basement. After all, offering the 'rents a little assistance is a nice way to say thanks for letting you have a party in the first place!

Countdown to a perfect party

1 MONTH OUT

☐ Check in with your parents on party dates, times and the number of guests.

3 WEEKS OUT

☐ Choose your party's theme and start making the invitations. Send them out a couple days later.

2 WEEKS OUT

☐ Gather party supplies and any crafting supplies necessary to make your décor elements.

1 WEEK OUT

☐ Follow up on any late RSVPs to get the final head-count and go grocery shopping with Mom.

2 DAYS OUT

☐ Plot out where your party will take place and hang up the decorations.

1 DAY OUT

☐ Clean the house and move any necessary furniture. Don't forget to plan your outfit.

DAY OF

☐ Lay out snacks and drinks, finalize décor and make any finishing touches. You're ready to party!

THEMES: INSTANT INSPIRATION

In the pages to come, we've provided you with a plethora of party themes to pick from. Of course, not every party has to have a theme, but a general idea can help inspire a busy hostess (that's you!) to set the scene, menu and décor scheme of what's sure to be a top-notch event. Picking a terrific theme at the start can actually make everything else easier. It doesn't have to be crazy complicated, either. Why not center a party around pizza or cookies? We do on page 47.

As far as activities go, each party we've outlined in this book includes a themed craft to make with your guests during the bash. Just gather enough supplies for each attendee, clear some space on the table or even the floor, and get crafting. It's the ultimate icebreaker: There's nothing like a hands-on activity to get guests talking. Plus, sharing in a creative DIY with your buds is bound to make for a totally amazing event.

THE GUEST LIST

Hooray, you're having a party! Before you get the word out to every kid in your grade, chat with Mom and Dad about the number of guests you can invite. If you've got limits, you'll need to make a guest list, focusing on friends who are sure to be fun additions and those who can get along well with almost everyone. Pick the pals you're closest with, not just the popular crowd. And if there's someone you'd like to get to know better? Invite her, too!

There might be a few people on your party guest wishlist that you just don't have room for, or people who have invited you to parties in the past but you don't feel the need to return the favor. Let's assume they'll probably find out about your bash, so the best policy is to be honest. If a classmate confronts you about being left off the list, gently explain that you would have liked to include them but that space was limited. It's likely they might be a little upset they weren't invited, but make alternate plans to hang out in the near future.

NICE TO MEET YOU

A truly successful hostess knows how to make a good introduction. After all, if you're bringing different groups of people together, it's probably true that the only person they'll have in common is Y-O-U. Make an effort to make thoughtful introductions to friends who might not hit upon their common interests right away. For example, explain to your school bud Becca that your camp pal Kirsten also loves ballet. Get them chatting about pirouettes and pointe shoes before you waltz off to make other fun and clever connections. Look at you, matchmaker!

RSVP

"RSVP" is a French acronym that stands for "répondez s'il vous plait," which means "please reply." As a hostess, it's key to know how many attendees you can expect. As a guest, it's polite to inform your hostess whether or not you can come to her party.

INVITES 101

Once you've got your guest list squared away, start formatting your invitations. You can pick up a pack of pretty printed invites from the store, send out an evite or craft your own. Whichever route you end up taking, the party invitation should inform guests of the following: where and when the party will take place (including start and end times), whether to bring gifts or not, what to expect and what to wear. It's also important to list your phone number or family email address so guests can RSVP by a certain date and let you know if they can make it. Don't forget to allow your pals enough time to mark their calendars. A good rule of thumb? Send out invitations two to four weeks before your event.

DARLING DÉCOR

Now for the fun part! Once you've decided on a date, guest list and theme, it's time to plan the party details. It's really the décor elements you include that can turn a regular hangout session into a stellar celebration. We're helping you with the specifics throughout the book, but here's a quick run-through of the basics.

• COLOR POP Pick a palette and stick with it. Keep it simple with two colors that appear throughout your party on things like plates, napkins, streamers and favors, or go all out and make a rainbow affair.
• STRIPES AND DOTS Easy design details can make a major impact on guests with minimal effort. Start with a polka-dotted invitation, pick up some striped straws and craft a garland out of cut paper circles. Instant cuteness.
• BOLD BACKDROP Consider a focal point for your party—normally the food or craft table—and create a standout backdrop. It can be as basic as bright balls of scrunched-up tissue paper taped to the wall in a grid or pattern, or something more complex, like the collection of pom poms on page 38.
• BABE ON A BUDGET We're not saying that you shell out tons of cash on supplies, especially when you can scour your house for cool centerpieces and other objects. A few of our (free) faves: Set out stacks of old books and pretty candles for a vintage look. Ask Mom to cut fresh flowers from the garden for a springtime scene. Wrap up empty boxes with holiday paper to create a festive Christmas centerpiece.

SERVE IT UP

Menu planning doesn't have to be as tricky as memorizing your French vocab. Choosing the bites and sips to serve at your party really depends on the type of event, theme and time of day your party is taking place. Having a 6 pm affair means you should offer guests some form of dinner (see our list of ideas below), while hosting a sleepover means you should definitely take breakfast into consideration.

The food you serve can help drive your theme home. You wouldn't dish up cereal at a luau, for example—you might want to bake a Hawaiian pizza instead, complete with ham and pineapple, and serve a tropical fruity punch. It can be fun to do a little light research to find the treats and snacks that coordinate with your chosen theme. Hit up the web or

NO-FAIL FOODS

A few go-to options that are always crowd-pleasers:

PIZZA Slice up a few selections, like veggie, extra cheese, pepperoni and even dessert pizza!

BURGERS AND HOT DOGS Ask Mom & Dad to fire up the grill, then take orders! Set out all the toppings on a tray and let guests dress their own.

POPCORN It's hard to go wrong with buttery, crunchy deliciousness. Add a seasonings bar like on page 133.

CHIPS AND DIP Potato chips and French onion dip, tortilla chips and salsa…it's easy to find a savory combo that fits with your party theme—and that partygoers will eat up.

ICE CREAM SANDWICHES Get creative by using home-made cookies as the sandwich and filling with fun ice cream flavors—bonus points if you make the ice cream yourself!

CUPCAKES Homemade cupcakes are surprisingly quick and easy. Try our recipe on page 147.

LEMONADE Doctor it up with lemon slices or a garnish of fresh mint as seen on page 139.

ROOT BEER Served in vintage cola bottles with cute straws? Perfect party go-to.

your local library and get cooking. We also provide you with a slew of tasty recipes to try in Chapter 6.

To help the party flow, set up the snacks, drinks and dessert stations in separate parts of the room. Spreading things out will encourage people to move around and mingle with other guests while they're helping themselves to all the yummy goodies you've provided, rather than everyone just parking themselves in front of the cake.

LET THE PARTY FLOW

Keep in mind: A good hostess should be dressed and ready to greet guests at least 15 minutes before party time. Our trick? Leave your shoes by the front door so you can run around to make the finishing touches before the doorbell rings. Do you have to don your best party dress? Definitely not. You'll probably be bouncing around all night, so steer clear of anything that's too fussy or uncomfortable. A comfy hostess puts everyone else at ease, too.

Ding-dong! Your first pals have arrived. Pop on a playlist (a must for party ambience), slip on your shoes and be sure to greet each guest and take their coats or bags. It's polite to make introductions to your parents, and if a new girl arrives whom your other friends don't know, be sure to introduce her to the party as well. While friends are filing in, offer up the food and drink options you've prepared, and let the mingling begin.

Once everyone has arrived, get the activities underway. We've outlined plenty of crafts you can do, but don't forget to have other forms of entertainment on hand, too. That can be anything from a movie that fits with your party's theme to board games or even old-school lawn games like tag, badminton or volleyball. The most fun parts of any party often take place during an awesome activity planned by an accomplished hostess. Yep, now that's you!

A FAITHGIRLZ! HOSTESS IS...

PREPARED She takes the time to plan a great party, and doesn't overwhelm herself by waiting 'til the last minute.

THOUGHTFUL She checks in with each guest to make them feel welcome and comfortable, and doesn't let the party revolve around her wishes alone.

GENEROUS She makes sure that there's enough food, drink and craft supplies to go around for all who want them.

FUN! She intends to have an awesome time at her own party, and helps each guest do the same.

Your Day-of Do's

Pre-party, consult this checklist to make sure
you're right on track.

❑ Have a healthy snack. Making sure you get some
protein before your party is key. Whip up a quick
PB&J and wash it down with some milk to fuel
up before the fun starts. A hangry hostess (that's
hungry + angry) is never a good idea!

❑ Make one last clean sweep. A few hours before the
party, straighten up any surfaces, put away any
breakable trinkets and give the room one final
dusting. Soon, your soirée setting will be sparkling!

❑ Lay out the treats. Make sure your sips & snacks
table is set well before the first friend arrives. You
don't want to be greeting guests with sticky hands!

❑ Plan time for pics. Build in time to take quick
snapshots of your party details: the décor you spent
hours crafting, the delish treats you slaved over
and the pretty favors you picked out. Having great
photos to remember your party by will make the
memories even sweeter.

Quiz!

WHAT'S YOUR SOIRÉE STYLE?

Are you the tea-party type or a boisterous-bash belle? Take our quickie quiz to determine your ultimate party style.

1. You're flipping channels on Sunday night. What sticks?
    a. A re-run of your fave rom-com.
    b. The laugh-out-loud sitcom show you watch on the regs.
    c. A special on planet Earth. Polar bears fascinate you.
    d. A reality competition. May the best girl win!

2. Who's closet would you steal in a heartbeat?
    a. Taylor Swift—she has the best collection of dresses.
    b. Selena Gomez—her style has just a little bit of edge to its sweetness.
    c. Lauren Conrad—a boho girl's dream come true.
    d. Zendaya—she's bold and not afraid to rock a look that's uniquely hers.

3. At a party, you're always the one…
    a. Making connections. Matchmaker is your middle name!
    b. Telling jokes. You love to get a good laugh.
    c. Bringing over freshly cut flowers from the yard.
    d. Starting the dance party, natch.

Mostly A's: YOU'RE A GARDEN PARTY GIRL
Your dreamy outlook deserves a romantic setting. From fresh florals to lush decor, a presh tea party held in a gorgeous garden is just your speed. Don't forget the flower crowns. Swoon!

Mostly B's: YOU'RE A MOVIE NIGHT MAVEN
You're always watching the latest flicks and you love to have a good time. Your bubbly and bright personality calls for a movie marathon—you'll catch up on the hottest films while having a good gabfest with your girls.

Mostly C's: YOU'RE A GLAMPING GAL
Your fondness for all things nature and your love of the outdoors means you're right at home in a tent under the stars. That casual style translates well to a backyard event. Gear up for a game of flashlight tag and gather 'round the bonfire: You're on s'mores duty.

Mostly D's: YOU'RE A DANCE PARTY DOLL
We know your dramatic tendencies mean we can almost always find you on the dance floor. Put yourself in charge of the playlist. Being in the spotlight is your specialty, and a rousing bash is your time to shine. Just remember to not step on anyone else's toes.

ANYTIME PARTIES

Why wait for a birthday or holiday to throw a bash?
Sometimes the "just because" parties are the best
ones. Gather a few key ingredients (good friends,
yummy food and a pom pom or two) and watch the
party magic happen. Keep these fun anytime get-
togethers super simple or go all out with stylish
touches. Invite two friends or twenty—it's your party!

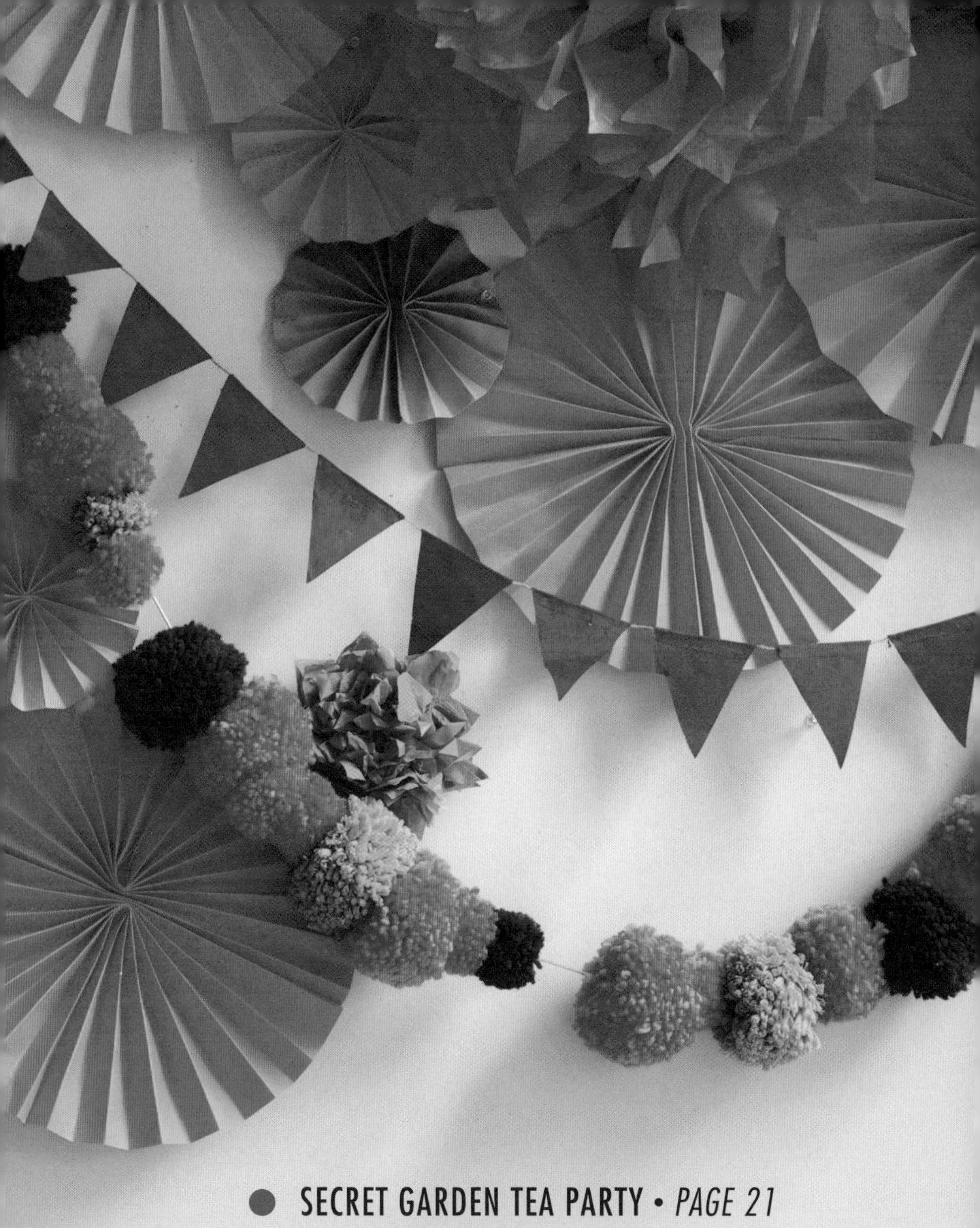

Secret Garden Tea Party

Have a ball hosting a bouquet brunch with all your belles.

Center your event on beautiful blooms and a ladylike menu. Declare it a flower potluck: Ask buds to bring a bunch of blossoms, which you'll use to make artful arrangements. Every girl will leave with a custom bouquet—a lovely reminder of your friendship.

SET THE SCENE
This out-of-doors event is especially fun in spring, but can be pulled off whenever the weather is warm. Keep an air of whimsy: This isn't your traditional tea party. Yep, it's fun to break out the pearls, lace and fine china, but why not rock your fave hot pink sneakers with your finest frock? Get dressed up without getting overdressed, and encourage your girls to do the same. Craft festive flower crowns for each attendee, and lay out the croquet set for a rousing lawn game under the sun.

INVITE INSPIRATION
Give guests a preview of the spring celebration to come by cutting petals out of cardstock. Pencil in the date, time and location on the back of your creation, along with an RSVP email address. Ask every girl to bring a bouquet of flowers, and add a hint about the dress here, too.

COLOR SCHEME
Seafoam and mint make a gorgeous pairing for an outdoor soirée. White lace plays second fiddle to the softer, cooler colors, and all three will ensure the rainbow of blooms your pals are providing will take center stage.

DÉCOR DREAMS
Keep things ladylike by asking Mom to lend the kitchen table and a few mix 'n' match chairs. Set up everything under a favorite tree in the backyard. A lace tablecloth can be easily found at a thrift shop, along with pretty napkins and serving trays. A pair of tall candlesticks adds a whimsical note.

TEACUP TERRARIUMS

Pretty vintage teacups filled with leafy succulents serve as the perfect take-home decorations. Scout local antique shops or Goodwill for an array of mismatched teacups, then plant delicate succulents and position on your tea table. At the end of the party, gift the tiny terrariums to guests as fun favors. Make these pretties up to a week in advance of your event.

[WHAT YOU'LL NEED]

Vintage porcelain teacups (1 for each guest) • Potting soil • Small succulents (find at your local florist or home improvement store: at least 1 per teacup)

[WHAT YOU'LL DO]

1. Wash and dry the teacups. Fill each up to ²/₃ height with potting soil.
2. Gently remove succulents from their packaging and lightly plant in soil, burying the root ball and securing plant in place.
3. Add more soil around base of plant to fill to teacup rim. Tidy up edges of each teacup with a damp paper towel.

SIPS AND BITES

Focus on light nibbles and bright berries as the main event for your brunch fare. Traditional treats like lemony crumb-topped muffins and crisp cucumber tea sandwiches are surprisingly simple to whip up. Add a refreshing twist by serving rose-scented iced tea and fresh-squeezed lemonade flavored with just a hint of mint. Sweet!

Menu

Tea Party

Triple Berry
Lemon Muffins*

Cucumber Cream
Cheese Rounds*

Fresh Berries and Yogurt

Rosewater Iced Tea*

Mint Lemonade*

** Find the recipes
in chapter 6*

BRILLIANT BOUQUETS

Indulge all your floral fantasies by crafting fanciful bouquets from the flowers your girls tote along. Provide each girl with a vase to take home, then pluck your favorite blooms and arrange at will!

[WHAT YOU'LL NEED]

At least three bunches of fresh flowers (any kind you like) • Tall glass vases or quart-sized mason jars • Scissors • Ribbon or trim

[WHAT YOU'LL DO]

1. Set the vase or jar on a sturdy tabletop surface. Select greenery like eucalyptus or leather leaf and trim stems to fit in vessel.
2. Begin to place the heavier blooms you're using, trimming stems so the blossom heads pop out just above the top of the vase.
3. Fill in gaps between blooms and add texture with smaller, more delicate blossoms, arranging for color and variety.
4. Tie a bright bow around the rim of your vase for a final flourish.

✳ Flower Arranging 101 ✳

4 THINGS TO REMEMBER

You don't have to be a master florist to create a gorge arrangement. Just follow these quick tips…

1. Work with stems in multiples of threes (could be colors, flower types or the number of blooms).

2. Start with leafy stems or greenery as a base for your bouquet.

3. Cut individual bloom stems so the head of each flower hits just at the top of your vase.

4. Less isn't always more. While bud vases highlight a single flower, larger jars benefit from a full-on floral frenzy.

Summer Spa Party

Soak up the sun, sit back and sip smoothies with your besties. So chill.

Set up your zen zone anywhere: in your backyard, bedroom or at a pal's pool. Then, get ready for a relaxing afternoon of face masks, mani-pedis and tropical refreshers.

SET THE SCENE
Go for an all-out pool party, asking guests to bring bathing suits and set up for a serious splash fest, complete with beach chairs and snacks served pool-side. Or keep things low-key with just a couple of friends lounging in your bedroom or backyard with a stack of magazines.

INVITE INSPIRATION
A casual evite is well-suited for this party, as friends tend to travel during the summer months and a mailbox is no substitute for an email inbox (hello, instant!). We heart sites like paperlesspost.com, where you can design your own invitations to match your party's theme. Need a hint? Try something with juicy popsicles or a splashin' pool scene. Fill in the date, time and location of your event, enter guests' email addresses, then track RSVPs online. Send text reminders to check inboxes so there's plenty of notice.

COLOR SCHEME
Keep the refreshing aquatic vibe going strong with cool blues, bright greens and crisp whites. Take inspiration from a pretty beach towel or fave bathing suit pattern, and then match plates, cups and napkins to those hues.

DÉCOR DREAMS
Collect all the bright towels and beach chairs you own to set up outside in a sunny spot, or transform your room into a blue-green oasis. Bonus points if you decorate a beach umbrella with a festive pom pom garland (see page 40). Make a real splash by stocking up on sunnies and flip-flops from the dollar store—pick out a coordinating pair for each pal.

LUXE LAVENDER SACHETS

Lavender is naturally relaxing. Gifting your girls with a sweet-smelling sachet is a thoughtful touch that will carry the spa theme home. They can bury the petite lavender pouch between stacks of T-shirts in their dresser drawers, or keep it on their nightstand to help them de-stress before bed. Perfect for calming any back-to-school jitters!

[WHAT YOU'LL NEED]

Small muslin drawstring bags (1 for each guest: find 'em on Amazon.com) • Dried lavender buds (enough to fill each bag; you can buy them online) • Pretty ribbon • Scissors • Hot glue gun

[WHAT YOU'LL DO]

1. Lay out the muslin bags on a table, smoothing them flat.
2. Trim the ribbon to fit the width of one bag, repeating for all bags.
3. Using the hot glue gun (and Mom's help, if necessary), apply a thin line of glue to the front of the bag and gently place the ribbon, smoothing any wrinkles. Repeat on all bags.
4. Cut small triangles from the length of ribbon and fold triangles to use to wrap each of the drawstrings to create tiny tassels on each end.
5. Once the glue has dried (about 5 to 10 minutes), fill each bag with a couple spoonfuls of lavender buds.
6. Pull drawstrings tight to close and tie securely with a knot.

LUSCIOUS AVOCADO FACE MASKS

Avocado is a natural way to get that summer glow. Double or triple the recipe depending on the number of guests—but it's best to make the masks in small batches. Prep these a few days ahead of your party to hand out to friends for instant application. Recipe makes 2 masks.

[WHAT YOU'LL NEED]

2 3-oz. glass jars with lids • 1 ripe avocado • ⅓ cup plain Greek yogurt • 2 tablespoons raw honey • 2 teaspoons fresh lemon juice

[WHAT YOU'LL DO]

1. Combine all ingredients in blender and blend together until no lumps remain, about 3 minutes. Turn off the blender in between pulses to scrape down sides of blender.
2. Pour mask into jars and tightly close lids. Refrigerate until party time. Note: Masks have a shelf life of ten days, so plan ahead to make in advance.
3. To use masks, apply a thick layer to your face and leave on for 10 to 15 minutes. Rinse with warm water.

Think crisp and clean when planning your spa party menu. Fresh ingredients prepared simply will cut down on stress for you—and ensure you'll feel fab poolside. Our Fruity Coconut Water Popsicles and bright Pineapple Watermelon Skewers add a blast of color to your party setting and will feel super refreshing on a hot day under the sun.

Menu

Spa Party

COOLING BENTO BOX:
Cucumber and Tzatziki,
Pineapple Watermelon
Skewers

Fruity Coconut Water
Popsicles*

Sweet Mango Mint
Smoothies*

*Find the recipes
in chapter 6*

CRAFT CLUB

PINK GRAPEFRUIT LIP BALM

This zingy citrus balm keeps your kisser super soft and adds a pretty tint, too. Get creative with your containers: Use an old Altoids Smalls tin or other tiny compact cases. This recipe makes eight small lip balms.

[WHAT YOU'LL NEED]

Lip balm tins (found on Amazon.com) • ⅓ cup coconut oil • 1 tablespoon Vitamin E oil • 1 tablespoon Jojoba oil • 20 drops pink grapefruit essential oil • 1 tube lipstick in any color (we chose a peachy coral)

[WHAT YOU'LL DO]

1. Roll up lipstick to the end and use a butter knife to slice off the stick. Place the lipstick and the coconut oil in a small bowl and melt in the microwave for 15 seconds.
2. Mix in the Vitamin E and Jojoba oil, then add the essential oil.
3. Stir well to combine, making sure there are no clumps of lipstick.
4. Pour into lip balm tins and let harden.

STAR STYLE!
join me for
a clothing
swap + fashion
shoot, we will
also change to

Star Style Swap

Take the runway! You'll have a blast trading threads and trying on the latest trends.

Invite your buds for a glam clothing swap and fashion show. Bonus: You'll donate the extra duds to a shelter in need.

SET THE SCENE
Style a star-studded, Old Hollywood-themed soirée where you'll trade clothes with your pals: It's like shopping without opening your wallet. Set up shop in your bedroom, stash a snack table in the kitchen and turn your hallway into a runway. Time for the walk-off? Dial up the tunes and get strutting!

INVITE INSPIRATION
Make a runway-ready invite with sparkling silver paper and teal layers— a silver pen keeps the color scheme in check. Ask each girl to bring over any clothes, shoes or accessories she no longer loves (old favorites, gently used threads or never-worn pieces). Cleaning out your own closet? A good rule of thumb: Get rid of any items you haven't worn in over a year. Don't forget to wash all your pieces before passing them on.

COLOR SCHEME
Silver and teal harken back to the glamorous vibe of Old Hollywood, where everything was glitzy and glittering. Stock up on silver tinsel stars and star-shaped confetti from the party store, cover the snack table in a teal cloth and look for star-bedecked plates, cups and napkins to fit the theme.

DÉCOR DREAMS
Channel your fave shop and morph your bedroom into a boutique. Set up clothing racks (find 'em at stores like Target) or spread garments out on your bed. Use bookshelves or side tables to lay out shoes and sweaters, and spread a blanket at the foot of your bed to display jewelry. Set out bins for donation items to make sure the leftover clothes and shoes go to good homes.

ROCKIN' RUNWAY
Ramp up your hallway into a catwalk, complete with front-row seating.

[WHAT YOU'LL NEED]

2 silver tinsel backdrops (grab them at a party store) • 2 curtains • Fishing line • Pushpins, tacks or gaffer's tape (found at Home Depot) • Floor pillows

[WHAT YOU'LL DO]

1. Find the best spot for your runway—ideally in a wide hallway. Make sure you have Mom and Dad's permission before attaching anything to the walls or the ceiling.
2. String up the tinsel backdrop at one end of the hall, using either gaffer's tape (which shouldn't remove paint!), pushpins or small tacks.
3. Hang a curtain on either side of the tinsel backdrop, stringing fishing line through them and attaching the fishing line to the wall or ceiling with pushpins, tacks or gaffer's tape.
3. Set out floor pillows for guests to sit on when they're not modeling.

SIPS AND BITES

Sweet and salty snacks are ideal for your clothing swap—gotta love no-mess nibbles guests can nosh on while perusing the racks or watching the fashion show. For stylish sips, pour sparkling water over scoops of lime sherbet for a bubbly refresher. Don't forget the striped straws.

Menu

Star Style Swap

Sweet and Spicy Candied Nuts*

Salted Caramel Brownies*

Star-Shaped Cookie Bars*

Chocolate-Dipped Strawberries

Lime Sherbet Floats

Find the recipes in chapter 6

STYLISH SUNNIES
Make like a moviestar and go glam with these stellar sunglasses.

[WHAT YOU'LL NEED]

Cat-eye sunglasses (1 pair for each guest) • Hot glue gun • Gems • Glittery star stickers • Small paper flowers • Small ribbon rosettes • Mini pom poms

[WHAT YOU'LL DO]

1. Spread out your embellishments and decide on the pattern you're going for. You can place decorations across the top frame of the sunglasses, down the sides or just in the corners.
2. Carefully use the hot glue gun to affix the embellishments in place, pressing down until the glue dries.

Pom Pom Party

So-pretty pom pom crowns steal the show at this colorful bash.
Don't forget the portrait session!

Deck out your dining room and transform it into a party wonder-land, complete with garlands, bunting and paper pinwheels. Set out plenty of yarn and scissors, and let the pom pom making begin.

SET THE SCENE
A crafting day at its core, the pom pom party is also a great excuse to get all dolled up. Pick a quiet Sunday, ask guests to don a party dress and settle in for a girly crafternoon complete with sweet snacks (and a good chat session).

INVITE INSPIRATION
Show off your own DIY skills by getting artsy on a store-bought invitation. Select a pretty pack of flat invites (not the folding kind) from the shelves and pick up a roll of pom pom trim from the fabric store. Measure the trim to fit around the perimeter of the card, then snip. Hot glue the trim to the back of the card, being careful to lay it flat. Hand deliver or slip the cards into your pals' lockers at school at least two weeks in advance.

COLOR SCHEME
A trio of brights turns heads. We had our hearts set on presh pink, turquoise blue and vibrant orange, but definitely add your favorite hue into the mix. Carry your colors into the yarn you choose for the crowns—you'll look per-fectly coordinated against the cute backdrop.

DÉCOR DREAMS
Ask for Mom's help to find the best backdrop for your party, then get going to make the decorations. Enlist your siblings (great for bonding time!) or a few close friends to help you snip, fold and tie your way to a stunning focal point. Cover a table with a bright cloth and arrange the snacks and drinks so there's plenty of room for pom pom making.

PAPER PINWHEELS

We love that you can repurpose these pretty pinwheels for a slew of other parties or give 'em to your buds on their way out. Make a range of sizes and colors for an eye-catching display.

[WHAT YOU'LL NEED]

Cardstock in your party's color scheme • Paper cutter • Small stapler or hot glue gun • Bone folder (tool to help make perfect creases: found at a craft store)

[WHAT YOU'LL DO]

1. Take one sheet of cardstock and begin to accordion fold in ½" folds until you reach the end of the paper. Use bone folder to get strong creases.
2. Pinch the stack of folds in the middle and bend to bring edges to meet. You're basically folding the stacks in half lengthwise to make a fan shape.
3. Repeat on a second sheet of cardstock.
4. Attach both fan shapes along edges by stapling or carefully hot gluing.

POM POM GARLAND

Post-party, this festive garland can easily find a new home in your bedroom. String it around your bedposts or drape it over a window for a fun flash of color.

[WHAT YOU'LL NEED]

Clover brand pom pom makers in 4 sizes (find them at a craft store) • Yarn in your party's colors (try for 3 to 4 colors) • 8' of metallic silver cord • Quilting needle • Scissors • Pushpins or adhesive hooks

[WHAT YOU'LL DO]

1. Follow the pom pom maker package instructions and begin to make pom poms for the garland. The number will vary, so start by making four of each color on each size pom pom maker.
2. Thread the quilting needle with the metallic cord. Begin threading pom poms on the needle, being careful to pierce each as close to the center as possible, and slide into place. Repeat for all pom poms.
3. Tie loops at each end of the metallic cord and use pushpins or adhesive hooks to hang in place.

YOU'RE INVITED

It's a pompom party!
for:
May 12 · 4 p.m.
date & time
My house
place
Sarah
hosted by:
Sarah@email.com
r.s.v.p.

TISSUE PAPER POMANDERS
These fluffy tissue paper poms look darling while decking out your walls.

[WHAT YOU'LL NEED]

Full sheets of tissue paper in your party's colors • Scissors • Pipe cleaners • Pushpins or adhesive hooks

[WHAT YOU'LL DO]

1. Take 8 sheets of tissue paper and begin to accordion fold in 1" folds until you reach the end of the paper.
2. Pinch stack of folds in middle and tie pipe cleaner around to hold in place.
3. Use scissors to trim edges of paper on either side into a point.
4. Begin to separate layers of tissue, gently fluffing out each one to make an evenly round ball shape.
5. Use tail of pipe cleaner to wrap around a pushpin or small adhesive hook.

   NOTE: For smaller pomanders, cut the tissue paper sheets in half and use only 6 sheets to accordion fold.

SIPS AND BITES

Keep the pom pom theme popping, even through your snack picks. Round treats add a fun twist to the standard party fare. Poke toothpicks with tiny pom poms purchased from the craft store, then spear them into donut holes for easy handling. Our Trailmix Popcorn Balls walk the line between salty and sweet—perfect for afternoon grazing.

Menu

Pom Pom Party

Trailmix Popcorn Balls*
Powdered Doughnut Bites
Sparkling Grapefruit Soda

* Find the recipe in chapter 6

POM POM CROWNS

Top off your event with a craft worthy of royalty. These tiaras take the flower crown to a whole new level of cool.

[WHAT YOU'LL NEED]

Clover brand pom pom makers in 4 sizes • Yarn in your party's colors (try for 3 to 4 hues) • Stretchy thin headbands (1 for each guest) • Scissors

[WHAT YOU'LL DO]

1. Follow the pom pom maker package instructions and begin to make pom poms for the crowns. The final number of pom poms will vary, so start by making 2 of each color on each size pom pom maker.
2. Keep the tie-off strings' ends long; you'll use these to attach your pom poms to the headband.
3. Arrange finished pom poms in the order you desire, then begin tying them on to the headband using the tie-off strings.
4. Perfect the placement, then cut any loose strings.

Cookie Bake-Off

Gather your girls for an afternoon of baking fun, then wrap up your wares and send them off to a local charity or your church's bake sale.

Stir up a batch of basic batter, and set out a cookie toppings bar for your crew to get creative. You'll be baking these goods for a charitable cause—but that doesn't mean you can't taste test. The most delicious concoction wins the cookie bake-off!

SET THE SCENE
Since you'll be gathered around the oven most of the day, the bulk of this party takes place in the kitchen. Stock your pantry beforehand with all the supplies you'll need, like cute cookie cutters and plenty of sprinkles. Round up a few retro aprons from thrift stores so each friend has one to wear.

INVITE INSPIRATION
Stick with the homemade theme and create your invite using brown kraft paper (or even a recycled paper bag). Layer on a circle of colorful printed cardstock or scrap paper and tie things off with a bow of bright cording or baker's twine. List the date and time of your event, then send them off at least two weeks in advance. Plan for a weekend afternoon: Parents will be out of the kitchen, so you'll have plenty of time to linger over your creations.

COLOR SCHEME
Channel a colorful French bakery and go for a rainbow of shades. Gather all Mom's best baking utensils—the more hues, the better!—and set out pretty bowls to host your array of cookie toppers on the counter. Then, get ready to hunker down for an afternoon of crafting treats for a good cause.

DÉCOR DREAMS
You'll need two stations: The counter works best for mixing, rolling and baking, while the kitchen table functions well for cooling, sorting and packing (so no worrying about making a mess while mixing the dough!).

COOKIE DOUGH

Sugar cookie dough serves as the basis for innumerable iterations of deliciousness. Make the dough ahead of the party so you have plenty of time for decorating.

[WHAT YOU'LL NEED] *Makes 4 dozen cookies*

2 ¾ cups flour • 1 teaspoon baking soda • ½ teaspoon baking powder • ¼ teaspoon salt • 1 cup or 2 sticks butter, softened • 1 ½ cups sugar • 1 egg • 1 teaspoon vanilla extract

[WHAT YOU'LL DO]

1. Preheat oven to 375°F. Line two baking sheets with parchment paper.
2. Sift together flour, baking soda, baking powder and salt in a small bowl, then set aside.
3. Using a stand mixer or hand mixer, cream together butter and sugar until fluffy. Beat in egg and vanilla.
4. Slowly work in dry ingredients in ½ cup increments until fully combined.
5. Gather the toppings in our Toppings Bar menu (see box on page 51) and let each friend come up with their own crazy combination. Sprinkle, roll or mix in cookie toppings. Note: Candy toppings work best if sprinkled on after baking but before cooling. Other toppings are generally OK to bake in, but ask Mom's advice if you're not sure.
6. When you're ready to bake, place rounded spoonfuls or balls of dough onto an ungreased cookie sheet, then bake for 8 to 10 minutes. Let stand on cookie sheet for 2 minutes before cooling on a wire rack.

Milk and cookies is a time-tested combo that will always please a hungry crowd. Serve up the milk with patterned straws in old-fashioned milk bottles or jelly jars trimmed with baker's twine. Don't forget to bake extra cookies ahead of time for guests to snack on while they work. And stock up on toppings like potato chips, pretzels and colorful candy—your girls are sure to sneak those!

CRAFT CLUB

TASTY TREATS

Small cookie boxes make for easy transport. Pick out tissue paper and pretty gift tags to match.

[WHAT YOU'LL NEED]

Small or medium bakers' boxes with lids • Tissue paper or parchment paper • Kraft paper gift tags and baker's twine • Markers

[WHAT YOU'LL DO]

1. Create the boxes according to directions.
2. Fill each box with a base layer of tissue paper or parchment paper.
3. Gently fill box with stacks of cookies, being careful not to crush them when you close the lid.
4. Write the cookie name and special ingredients on a gift tag, and use the twine to wrap around box.
5. Deliver your freshly baked goods to a shelter, church or local charity.

Cookie Bake-Off Toppings Bar

SOME TRULY TERRIFIC TOPPINGS: Here are our picks, but don't be afraid to try your own…

- Crushed pretzels
- Oreo crumbs
- Smashed potato chips
- Froot Loops
- Crushed graham crackers
- Mini marshmallows
- Mini M&Ms
- Nerds
- Gummy bears

BIRTHDAY PARTIES

A birthday party is about celebrating the guest of honor, so keep her faves in mind when planning these soirées (and if it's you, all the better!). We love honoring old traditions, but we're all for making new ones, too, like blowing out those candles on top of the best ice cream sundae you can dream up, or having a gab fest in a teepee under the stars. Get creative!

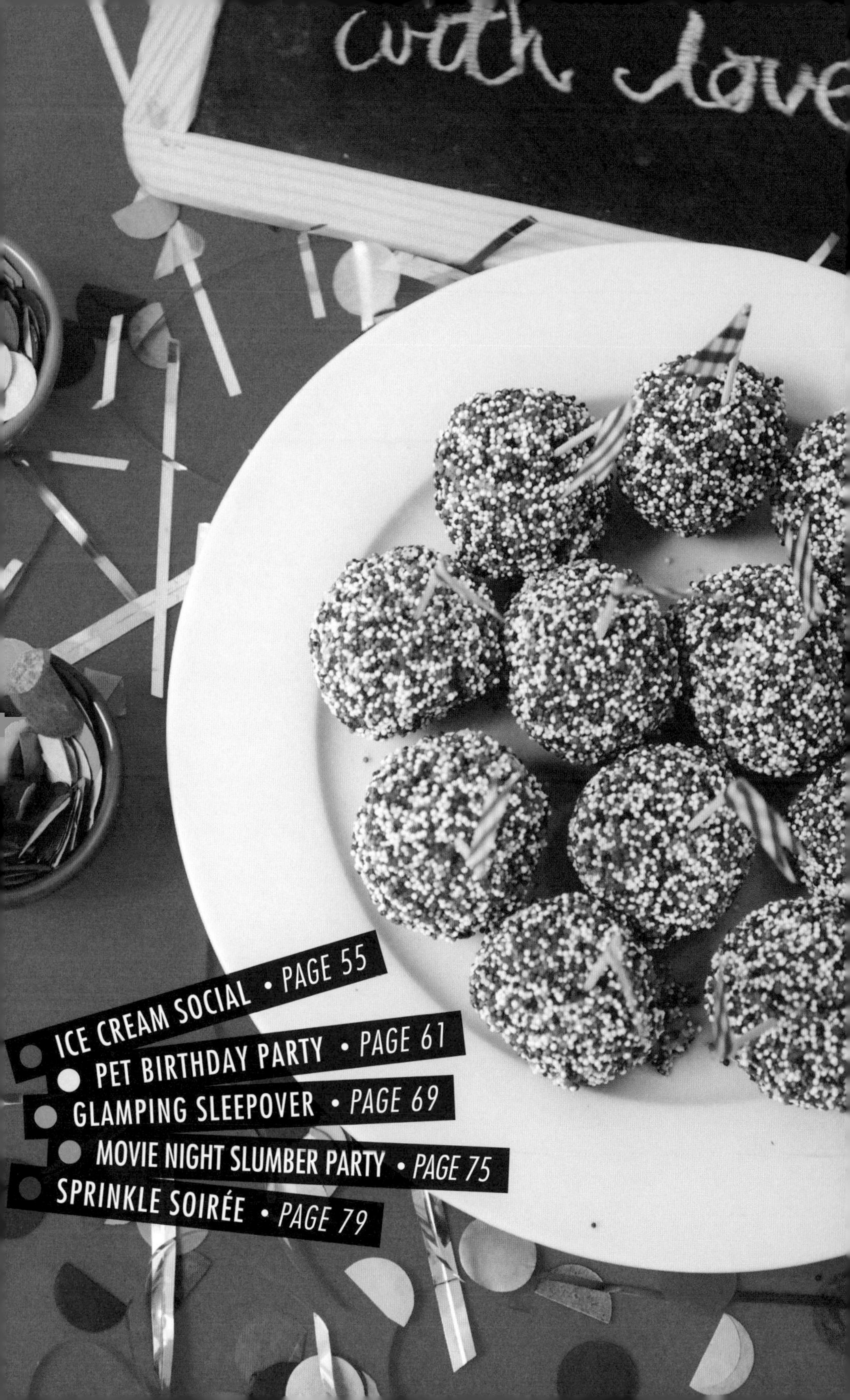
with love

Ice Cream Social

An old-fashioned ice cream social is just the thing for
a delightful (and delicious) birthday.

Invite all your pals for a relaxed Sunday spent making, well, sundaes!
Guests will have a blast concocting their signature mix-in blend—
they'll test it out at the party and each fill a jar to take home.

SET THE SCENE
Deck out the dining room with ribbons and add stripes of bright paint on
the party supplies to channel the sweet treat with a double-dipped theme.
Hit play on a fun pop playlist, whip up some party hats and make sure your
table is set—don't dish out the ice cream until the guests have arrived.

INVITE INSPIRATION
A painterly postcard invite is a cinch when you're already working with
acrylic for the other party crafts. Keep the drippy theme going strong by
making a couple brush strokes at the edges of a 6" square card. Tuck the
postcards into friends' lockers or mailboxes, or deliver them in person
a couple weeks before the party date.

COLOR SCHEME
Think sorbet and sherbet shades: strawberry pink, creamsicle orange, blue
raspberry, lemon yellow. The fruity hues lend a bright and cheerful vibe
that'll transform any setting. Stock up on craft paint in the same colors for
the décor items you'll be making pre-party.

DÉCOR DREAMS
Bypass the traditional bunting in favor of a hanging ribbon backdrop: cut
varying lengths of 2" wide ribbon, tie ribbons onto a 6' piece of twine and
pin twine ends to the wall behind your table—major impact for minimal
effort. Fill glass vases with white hydrangea blooms that mimic soft scoops
of ice cream (set them in bright paper cones to match the party hats).

PAINT-DIPPED TASTING SPOONS

A simple paint stroke makes these tiny wooden spoons a million times more adorable. Want to get creative? Try your hand at small stripes or bitty polka dots.

[WHAT YOU'LL NEED]

A pack of wooden tasting spoons (found at a party store) • Craft paint in your party's color scheme • Small bristle paintbrush • Wax paper

[WHAT YOU'LL DO]

1. Lay out a piece of wax paper on a flat surface and place spoons on top.
2. Dab a small amount of one color of paint onto a corner of the wax paper, then lightly dip brush in it.
3. Apply paint to spoon's handle, stopping about 1" below spoon's base.
4. Repeat for all colors and spoons. Let dry for 2 hours, and repeat on reverse.

PAINTED PARTY HATS

Present your pals with these bright and bold hats, each topped off with a painted stripe and a feathery pom pom.

[WHAT YOU'LL NEED]

Large sheets of square cardstock in your party's color scheme • Stapler or hot glue gun • Craft paint in your party's color scheme • Small bristle paintbrush • Feather boa • Small hole punch • Elastic string • Scissors

[WHAT YOU'LL DO]

1. Cut cardstock across the diagonal so you're left with 2 triangles.
2. Curl ends of one triangle in toward each other to create a cone shape. Staple or hot glue in place, making sure base of cone is large enough to wear.
3. Dip paintbrush in a small amount of paint and make a stripe along bottom edge of hat. Let dry while you make more hats.
4. Once paint is dry, cut a 5" piece of the feather boa and tie into a knot several times so it makes a small ball shape.
5. Hot glue feather boa pom pom to top of hat and repeat for all hats.
6. Use the hole punch to make a hole near bottom on opposite sides of hat.
7. Measure a piece of elastic string that fits snugly around your chin. Cut and thread through holes, tying knots to secure.

IT'S AN ICE CREAM SOCIAL!
SATURDAY MAY 25th 2PM
LEAH'S HOUSE ⟵

PLEASE RSVP: VANILLA FAN @
MAIL.COM

HOPE YOU CAN JOIN US!

CRAFT CLUB

MIX-IN MIXTURES

Make a mix-in bar that moves way beyond traditional sundae toppings—
see ya, hot fudge and cherries.

[WHAT YOU'LL NEED]

Mini peanut-butter filled chocolate cups • Nerds or other small candy • Mini
M&Ms • Gummy bears • Toffee crumbles • Rainbow sprinkles • 4 oz. jars with
lids • Round stick-on labels • Markers

[WHAT YOU'LL DO]

1. Set out your toppings in small bowls on the main food table. Don't forget
   to include spoons.
2. Give each guest a jar and lid to create their own mix-in mixture.
3. Write names of each friend's mix on a round label, then stick to lid of jar.
4. For the mix-in, set out a medium bowl with the guest's preferred ice cream
   flavor. Using two large spoons, mix in a couple spoonfuls of their mixture,
   using spoons to blend mixture into ice cream.
5. Scoop mixed ice cream into an ice cream cone, and present to your guest.

SIPS AND BITES

Dish up at least three ice cream flavors
for guests to choose from. We scooped
chocolate fudge, strawberry and mint
chocolate chip. It's helpful to have a
separate ice cream scoop for each
flavor—no mixing!

☁Menu

Ice Cream Social

Ice Cream Mix-ins Bar

Pink Chocolate-Dipped
Waffle Cones*

Root Beer Floats*

*Find the recipes
in chapter 6*

Pet Birthday Party

Both you and your furry friend will have a blast celebrating a milestone birthday with humans and animals alike.

Invite all the pets you know (and their owners) for an afternoon complete with treats for good tricks, toys and tiaras—one for each animal. You'll craft a fun backdrop for pet portraits. Start snapping!

SET THE SCENE
A casual ambience is paws-itively perfect for a pet party. Turn on some dance music, make sure there's easy outdoor access for the dogs to run around, and let everyone burn off some energy. Have plenty of balls and toys around for four-legged friends to play with (and extra leashes just in case). Once everyone is spent, head inside to craft pet crowns and take some photos of your favorite canines and felines.

INVITE INSPIRATION
Dig up a treasured photo of Fido or Whiskers to use as the main image for your invitation. Print copies and glue to a piece of patterned paper. Affix photo and border to cardstock with enough room to write your party details, instructing guests to bring their pets for a tail-waggingly good time.

COLOR SCHEME
Let your favorite colors inspire your party's color palette, but be sure to focus on brights so those furry coats will pop against your backdrop. Keep the treats table feeling sunny with a healthy dose of happy yellow.

DÉCOR DREAMS
Lay out a table with the bites, snacks and sips you'll be serving, and spread out the crown crafting supplies on another free table. A few floor pillows serve as comfy seating for pets and people in need of some relaxation time. Collect costume jewelry, faux glasses and bow ties as wardrobe options for your pet portrait photo shoot. Dole out the duds as pet-friendly favors.

CHEVRON PHOTO BACKDROP

Rows of tissue paper chevron stripes make any space feel festive, while a Happy Birthday garland of cutout letters anchors the backdrop. Save the chevrons to tape up in your bedroom after the party.

[WHAT YOU'LL NEED]

A large paper grocery bag • Pencil • Ruler • Scissors • Full-size sheets of tissue paper (about 20" x 30") in 5 colors • Painter's tape • Happy Birthday garland

[WHAT YOU'LL DO]

1. Cut along the seams of the paper bag to open it up and lay flat. Draw a triangle template onto a corner of the bag, being sure the side lengths are equal, and cut it out.
2. Use the triangle template to trace a larger chevron template along the full length of the paper bag. Begin to trace the triangle onto the bag near the edge, and continue moving the triangle horizontally to add more triangles in line with the first. Connect the lines so they make a continuous row. Add a 2" border to the bottom of the chevron template so you'll have enough room to overlap the strips when you tape them to the wall. Cut out the chevron template.
3. Unfold 4 sheets of tissue paper, making sure the edges are still aligned. Use the pencil to trace the chevron template onto the tissue paper, then cut through all 4 sheets. Repeat until you have 16 chevron strips in each color of tissue paper—or more, if you want it taller.
4. Tape up each chevron strip one at a time on your chosen wall, starting at the bottom where the wall meets the floor. Then begin to overlap the chevron strips, carefully taping one on top of the other until you've completed your backdrop.
5. Use pushpins to tack up your Happy Birthday garland in the center of the backdrop, then center your first pet, grab the camera and start shooting!

DOG AND CAT CROWNS

These charming crowns will look adorable atop your pets' heads.

[WHAT YOU'LL NEED]

Felt sheets in different colors • Hot glue gun • String or yarn • Scissors •
Quilting needle • Thread

[WHAT YOU'LL DO]

1. Use a piece of string or yarn to roughly measure the circumference of your
   pet's head, then cut. Lay cut string against a piece of felt: this is the length
   of your crown.
2. Cut out a crown pattern from felt piece that matches length of string,

and repeat with a piece of felt in a different color. Hot glue 2 pieces of felt together, matching up crown points.

3. Use quilting needle and thread to sew vertical edges together to make a complete circle.

4. Whipstitch 2 felt pieces together all the way around your crown. It's OK if your stitches aren't perfect—that'll make it all the more precious.

5. Using another piece of felt, cut out the number of years your pet is turning, and use quick stitches to sew it onto the front of your crown.

NOTE: Make a paper feather crown by using the paper feather tutorial on page 100 and attaching them to a paper band that fits the size of your pet's head.

The top dog menu items of your event will probably be the made-from-scratch dog biscuits and cat treats that your pet pals will gobble up. As for people food, dish up animal crackers and cake pops (it is a birthday party, after all!).

Menu

Pet Birthday

FOR PETS

Bone Up Dog Biscuits*
Starfish Cat Treats*
(plus plenty of fresh water)

FOR PEOPLE

Cake Pops
Animal Crackers
Pomegranate Juice with Seltzer

** Find the recipes
in chapter 6*

✳ Every Day Is a Party! ✳

INSTA-PARTY IDEA

Round up your buds for a spontaneous soirée, sock-hop style. Ask pals to rock their craziest socks, turn up retro tunes (we like Buddy Holly!) and break out some old-school board games (try Sorry!). Serve grilled PB&J sandwiches with ice-cold milk on the side.

Glamping Sleepover

Gather 'round the bonfire for a birthday bash filled with sweet s'mores, cozy quilts and late night campfire tales.

Grab your besties for a night spent under the stars. Ask each girl to come ready for some "glamorous camping"—you'll bring along the comforts of home as you brave the outdoors. Spend the day whipping up a cute friendship quilt with your girls to commemorate the event.

SET THE SCENE
Set up camp in the backyard on a clear afternoon. This party calls for a tongue-in-cheek twist on traditional camping—bring out string lights, an iPod dock and plenty of pillows to set a cozy glam ambience. Don't forget to gather long sticks for marshmallow roasting.

INVITE INSPIRATION
If you're short on notice, shoot off a quick camping-themed evite, but if you've got a longer lead-time, try searching around the local thrift stores or antique shops for kitschy vintage postcards featuring scenes of the great outdoors. Inscribe your party details on the postcards' reverse side for a fun twist on the traditional invite. Be sure to set a rain date, just in case!

COLOR SCHEME
Stick with classic plaid elements and colors like red, navy, green and yellow. Throw in some bright pink for good measure—it'll instantly up the glam factor. A few gold or metallic accents lend a luxe vibe as well.

DÉCOR DREAMS
Glamping means your campsite is fully equipped with cozy musts like sheepskin throws, cozy rugs and plush pillows (lay out a tarp first!). Rustic elements such as wooden crates and woven baskets help give the party a chic outdoorsy feel. Before you start ransacking the house, ask Mom for approval on what could survive one night in the wilderness (er, your backyard).

LOVELY LACE TEEPEE

Sweeping layers of lace make for a graceful canopy and serve as a dreamy backdrop for your glamping party. Just make sure it's a warm night if you're planning on actually sleeping outside.

[WHAT YOU'LL NEED]

2 large vintage lace tablecloths or curtains about 60" x 80" (try Goodwill) • Sewing machine • 6 yards of pom pom trim • 4 8' wooden dowels or PVC pipes • Twine • 4 large feathers • Adhesive Velcro strips • Scissors

[WHAT YOU'LL DO]

1. Cut one of the lace cloths diagonally down the middle, leaving you with two large triangles.
2. Lay one triangle on the floor with short side facing you and diagonal side on the left. Place uncut lace cloth next to the long vertical side of triangle. Place second triangle's vertical side on opposite side of uncut lace cloth, leaving you with a trapezoid shape. This is how you'll sew the teepee cover.
3. Using the sewing machine and with Mom's help, sew trapezoid pieces together in the order you laid them out.
4. Cut pom pom trim in half and sew on trim to the outside diagonal edges.
5. Gather your 4 dowels and hold them together at the top. Tie a piece of twine around to temporarily hold while you spread out and position feet into a stable square shape. Use another piece of twine to tightly wrap tops of dowels and tie off.
6. Drape the teepee cover over the 4 dowels or PVC pipes, using the pom pom trimmed sides to mark the opening.
7. Remove backing from an adhesive Velcro strip and stick on lace at the top of the dowels to keep teepee cover closed.
8. Tie together 4 feathers using twine, and place on top of your teepee.

✳ Every Day Is a Party! ✳

INSTA-PARTY IDEA

Love the great outdoors? Gather your girls for a morning hike: Pick a path through a local park, look for woodland creatures and whistle while you walk. Then head back home for fresh fruit smoothies and bowls of steel-cut oatmeal with tasty toppings.

SIPS AND BITES

Take your traditional s'mores setup to new heights by filling the sweet sandwiches with homemade (pink!) marshmallows and three kinds of chocolate. Purists will still love graham crackers, but throw in pretzel chips and chocolate chip cookies as contenders as well. In the morning, ask Dad to fire up the camp stove for sizzling bacon and eggs.

Menu

Glamping Sleepover

Puffy Pink Marshmallows*

Stellar S'mores bar

Real Root Beer

*Find the recipe
in chapter 6*

FRIENDSHIP QUILT

In true *Sisterhood* style, craft a cheery quilt that each girl will sign with a sweet friendship memory. Post-party, pass the quilt around for a few weeks spent on each pal's bed.

[WHAT YOU'LL NEED]

7 yards of fabric in 6 different colors/patterns • Straight pins • Full size bed-sheet (as backing) • Full size blanket (as batting) • Sewing machine • Yarn that matches the bedsheet color • Quilting needle • Scissors • Fabric markers

[WHAT YOU'LL DO]

1. Cut 9 10" squares of each of your fabrics.
2. Lay out the squares in rows of 6 to form your quilt design. Ours featured one square of each fabric in each row, arranging so that no like fabrics were touching. Take a picture of your layout in case you need to reference it later.
3. Ask Mom to help you with the sewing machine, and begin sewing each square in each row together. Then join rows by sewing the rows together. This forms the top of your quilt.
4. Lay quilt down on a flat surface, right side up. Lay sheet with right side facing quilt. Lay blanket down on top of sheet, and trim blanket and sheet to fit perimeter of the quilt, if necessary.
5. Use the sewing machine to sew quilt, sheet and blanket together on 3 sides of the perimeter, leaving fourth side open.
6. Place the blanket inside the quilt through open end, feeding it into corners so that it's flush.
7. Hand sew open end of quilt. Then, lay quilt face up on a flat surface.
8. Cut a piece of yarn about 7 ½' long. Thread quilting needle with yarn. Place a stitch through middle of first square on the top row, going up through bottom and bringing it back down. (This holds blanket in place.)
9. Using same thread, place another stitch through the middle of next square in the row, moving down length of quilt. Repeat until you've placed a stitch in every square in that row.
10. Cut thread joining stitches between the squares, leaving each square with 2 5" strings. Tie knots between 2 strings, then trim string ends to approximately 1" long.
11. Repeat across all squares and all rows.

Movie Night Slumber Party

Host a classic movie night sleepover for your closest crew, complete with popcorn, pillow fights and a pretty make-your-own tote craft.

Lights, camera, action! You're calling the shots on a cinematic-worthy sleepover. Your masterpiece? The amazing indoor fort you'll snuggle up in to watch some flicks and catch up on (non-Hollywood) gossip.

SET THE SCENE
Stake out the best spot for your movie-watching marathon, and then claim the family room or the basement as your territory for the night. Make sure there's room for your popcorn bar and plenty of space to spread out your supplies for the trimmings totes you'll create together.

INVITE INSPIRATION
Invite friends to your birthday bash with a movie-themed evite sent out two weeks in advance of the big day. Search for flick-inspired themes, like a bag of buttery popcorn, a movie slate outlining the party name details or a theater ticket listing the date and time.

COLOR SCHEME
Let your event's color scheme be determined by the shades of the bedding you gather for the fort—more on that below. If your blankets and sheets are on the cooler side, say blues and greens, throw in a dash of pink (faux fur pillows perhaps?) to warm things up and you're set.

DÉCOR DREAMS
Rope in the sibs to help you gather clean sheets, pillows and blankets from all over the house (with Mom's OK, of course!) to build an awesome blanket fort. Use dining room chairs as the supports for your fort, then begin to drape, tuck and fold sheets and blankets into a makeshift tent. String up Christmas lights inside for a festive glow, and fill the tent with pillows and comfy blankets. Then, settle in for a night of noshing and Netflix.

TRICKED-OUT POPCORN BAGS

A quick strip of tape makes a brown paper bag instantly adorable.

[WHAT YOU'LL NEED]

Medium brown paper lunch bags • Scissors • Washi tape in multiple colors/patterns (that's Japanese paper tape, found at a craft store)

[WHAT YOU'LL DO]

1. Cut the tops of the paper bags so they stand approximately 6" tall.
2. Cut a piece of Washi tape to fit the length of the front of the bag, and affix tape to bag.
3. Repeat step 2, creating stripes of Washi tape along front of bag.
4. Right before guests arrive, fill bags with popcorn.

SIPS AND BITES

Move aside, butter. The traditional toppings for your fave movie snack just got way more interesting. From cocoa chili to cool ranch to cinnamon sugar, these fun flavor combos will take popcorn from boring to award-winning in just one shake.

Menu

Movie Night Slumber Party

Popcorn Seasoning Spices*

Vintage Cola

Pizza

Find the recipe in chapter 6

Sprinkle Soirée

Perfect for a surprise birthday, get ready to sprinkle
the girl of the hour with love!

● ● ●

Gather all the ingredients for a super sweet sprinkle soirée: a collection of confetti big and small, the makings for a sparkling snow globe —and a group of friends in on the surprise.

SET THE SCENE
Pick the day of your bud's birthday (or a couple days before) for a fun get-together at your house. Hint: Ask a few friends for help in getting the guest of honor there without cluing her in to the party plans. Before the bash, craft a playlist of her top tunes, decorate your space in her fave hues and serve up her go-to snacks. Find a spot for everyone to hide and flick off the lights. When she walks in, yell, "Surprise!" and cover her in confetti!

INVITE INSPIRATION
Snag a pack of pre-printed invitations and personalize them by filling each envelope with a handful of paper confetti. Pencil in the where and when, being sure to spell out that it's a secret. Allow at least three weeks for your guests to save the date…surprise parties require a bit more planning.

COLOR SCHEME
Go color crazy with a rainbow of hues to fit the sprinkle theme, but pick one main color—ideally her favorite—to tie everything in. Fun extras like bright straws anchored in a confetti-filled jar help your snack table pop.

DÉCOR DREAMS
Transform the living room into party central with a confetti wall. Score parental permission first, then get the sprinkle shower started by scattering around a light coating of confetti before the guests arrive—you'll want to give the space a party feel. Our tip? Stock up on paper confetti cut into larger pieces (or make your own)—way easier when it comes time to clean up.

MAKE IT

CONFETTI WALL BACKDROP
This quick craft turns a regular room into a life-size confetti world.

[WHAT YOU'LL NEED]

Cardstock in 6 to 8 bright colors • Circle cutter (try your local craft store) • Self-healing cutting mat • Painter's tape • Scissors • Double-stick tape

[WHAT YOU'LL DO]

1. Choose a piece of cardstock and set it on top of the cutting mat.
2. Set the circle cutter to make 4" rounds. Place the circle cutter on top of the cardstock and begin to cut out circles, being sure to account for the best use of the paper—no wasted space.
3. Repeat for the other colors of cardstock you've chosen, until you have at least 6 rounds of each color.
4. Cut a loop of double-sided tape to affix the back of one of the circles to the wall (get Mom's permission).
5. Repeat for rest of the rounds, varying the spacing by overlapping the circles slightly or spreading them out with plenty of space in between each dot.

SIPS AND BITES

A tiered confection covered in colorful sprinkles really takes the, um, cake. Serve slices on bright plates alongside bottles of sparkling fruit sodas complete with stylin' straws. Round things out with a pretty platter of decorated doughnut holes (use matching sprinkles or mix it up with colored sugars).

Menu

Sprinkle Soirée

Sprinkle Cake*
Doughnut Holes
Fizzy Sodas
Her Favorite Snacks

Find the recipe in chapter 6

SPARKLING SNOW GLOBES

Channel the celebratory vibe into an adorable animal snow globe that shakes things up long after the party's over—and is super simple to make.

[WHAT YOU'LL NEED]

Gold spray paint • Plastic toy animals (1 for each guest) • Hot glue gun • 16 oz. glass jars with lids • Water to fill • Glitter • Metallic confetti

[WHAT YOU'LL DO]

1. Ask a parent or an older sib to help you spray paint animals on all sides. Let dry overnight—it's best to do this step in advance of the party.
2. Place animal right side up on underside of jar lid. Use hot glue gun to stick animal's feet firmly in place.
3. Fill bottom of jar with a couple tablespoons or so of glitter and confetti. Fill rest of jar with water.
4. Screw on lid tightly, then shake your new snow globe.

✳ Every Day Is a Party! ✳

MINI SCHOOL SURPRISES

3 quick, easy (and free!) ways to wow your bestie—even if it's not her birthday.

1. PAL POTLUCK Treat your BFF to her fave lunch. Assign friends to each bring a portion of a potluck meal, complete with cloth napkins and real silverware. Fancy!

2. THREE OF A KIND Pick a day to all dress in your bud's go-to outfit, then take plenty of samesies photos.

3. LOCKER LOVE Deck out a friend's locker door in wrapping paper, bows, cute pics and all things sparkly—just because you heart her.

HOLIDAY PARTIES

Whether it's red hearts, pastel Easter eggs or gold tinsel, holiday parties can always evoke classic elements, but there's definitely room for your own spin. Throw a pink and gold New Year's Fête, have an indoor Easter picnic or DIY your own cute Christmas sweaters. Turn the page—we've got everything you need to host the event of the season.

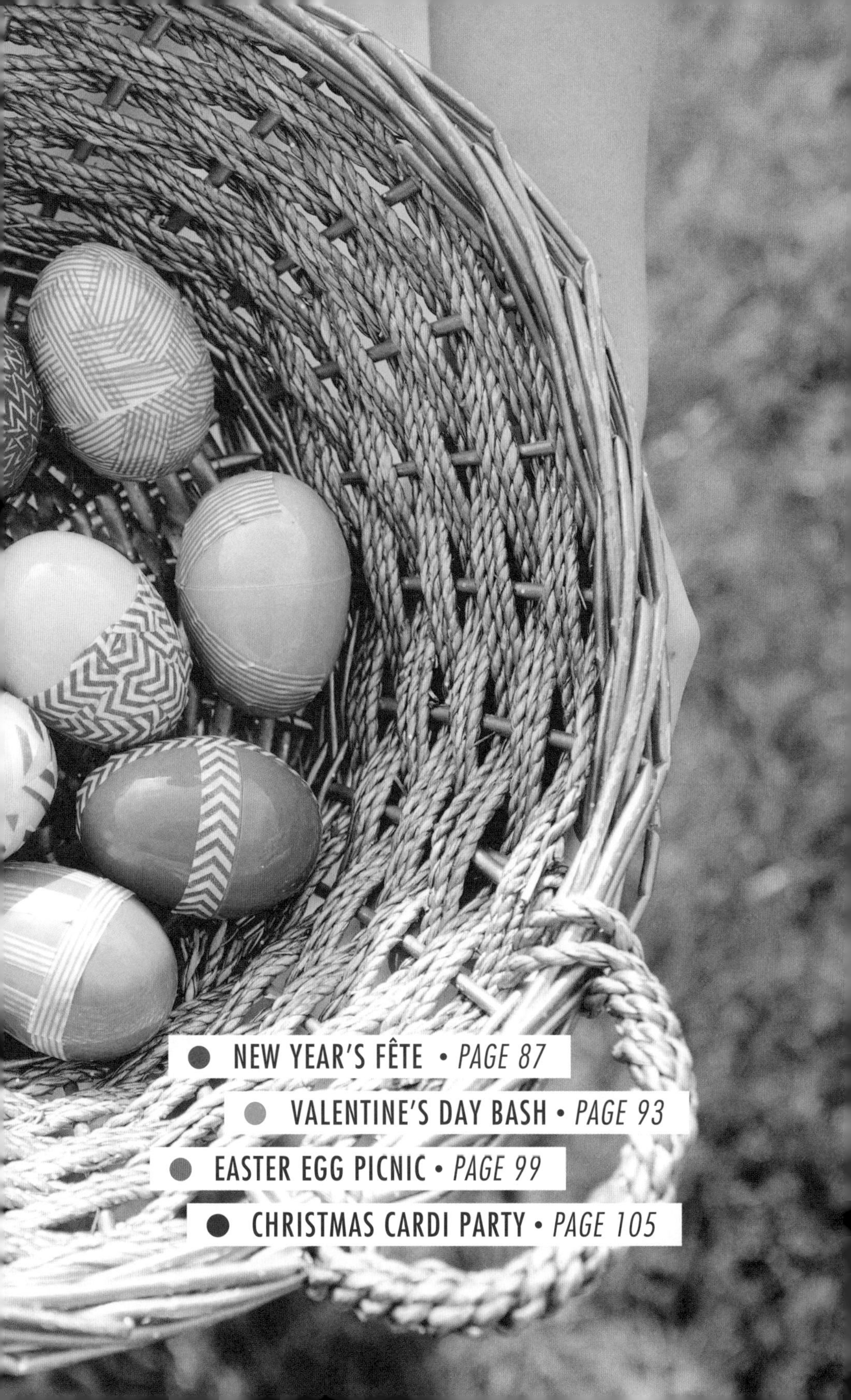

New Year's Fête

Ring in the New Year right with good friends, cute party hats and an inspiring collage craft.

Picture this: A New Year's celebration, surrounded by fondue, friends and family. Envision your new goals, hopes and dreams on a chalkboard collage while fêting the year gone by. Happy New Year!

SET THE SCENE
Look for a clean slate setting that you can make totally your own, like a plain wall in your house, the basement or even a tidied-up garage. Spend holiday break prepping: Compile a NYE playlist, gather all the glittering confetti you can find and stock up on noisemakers for a rousing midnight welcome.

INVITE INSPIRATION
Now's your chance for all-over sparkles: a sequined card feels ultra luxe—find it at your craft store or DIY by covering a piece of cardstock in a thin coating of glue and sequins. Pair it with a layer of black paper and use a gold marker to scribble out your party deets. Hand deliver your pretty invites, or snap a photo and share with guests on social media to spread the word.

COLOR SCHEME
Skip the standard black/silver and shoot for something that feels of-the-moment, like shocking pink and glittering gold. Anything metallic will look instantly glam—perfect if you're setting up in a raw space like the basement.

DÉCOR DREAMS
A floating fringe backdrop brings the drama. Center two side tables in front, each anchored with a fondue pot and covered in a metallic gold cloth. (Snag a few yards from the fabric store.) Pick up some shiny plates and pink napkins, and tie sparkling cider coupes with shimmery pink bows. Party horns help ring in the new year right!

PARTY HAT HEADBANDS

Hats off to the New Year with this glittery topper. Craft one for each of your festive friends.

[WHAT YOU'LL NEED]

10" square sheet of pink cardstock • Hot glue gun and glue sticks • Gold tinsel garland • Thin plastic headband • Scissors

[WHAT YOU'LL DO]

1. Cut cardstock in half along diagonal. Roll one of the resulting triangles into a cone shape and use dots of hot glue along edges of seam to hold in place.
2. Cut a length of tinsel garland to fit around bottom perimeter of the cone, then hot glue in place along the outer bottom.
3. Tie a small knot of tinsel garland until it makes a ball shape. Stuff a small part of ball inside tip of hat and use glue gun to attach ball to top of hat.
4. Cut two horizontal slits ¼" away from bottom of hat and thread headband through slits. Add 2 drops of glue to inside bottom of hat where headband will sit. (Slightly off-kilter is cute!) Press in place until set.

SIPS AND BITES

It's tradition to serve up sizzling fondue and tasty dippers as a celebratory snack during New Year's festivities. Set out apple wedges, slices of baguette and torn pumpernickel bread pieces, broccoli florets, celery, red pepper sticks and baby carrots for dipping into the warm cheese fondue. On another platter, banana coins, mini cookies, pound cake pieces and fresh strawberries turn into a dream dessert when dipped in melty chocolate fondue. Toast midnight with decorated cups filled to the brim with sparkling apple cider.

Menu

Cheesy Fondue and Dippers*

Chocolate Fondue and Dippers*

Sparkling Apple Cider

* Find the recipes in chapter 6

INSPIRING COLLAGE CHALKBOARDS

The secret for resolution success? A pretty inspiration board inscribed with your New Year's goals.

[WHAT YOU'LL NEED]

Mini chalkboards (snag 'em on Amazon.com) • Old magazines • Scissors • Elmer's glue • Colored chalk

[WHAT YOU'LL DO]

1. Grab a stack of old magazines and some scissors. Cut out anything you find inspiring—a fashion photo, meaningful quote, fun headline—whatever strikes your fancy. Snip everything you're drawn to (no questioning it!).
2. Arrange your clippings onto the front of your chalkboard and glue into place, any way you like.
3. Use the chalk to write out your goals, hopes, resolutions and dreams for the New Year. Hang the board over your desk or in your locker.

Valentine's Day Bash

Spend the afternoon folding beautiful origami valentines with your lovelies. As for who you'll give them to? That's up to you!

Celebrate Valentine's Day with a pink and red party complete with heart-filled cupcakes. What's not to love?

SET THE SCENE

Claim the dining room as yours for the day. You'll need lots of space for folding the origami, along with plenty of room for a pink and red candy bar. A few days before the bash, put together a playlist with songs that have a pink, red or love theme. Ask friends to submit their faves, too.

INVITE INSPIRATION

Make an origami-inspired invitation by cutting out symmetrical hearts from printed cardstock and folding them in half. Arrange hearts on a piece of plain cardstock. Once in place, glue down one side of the folded heart to the card, leaving the other side unattached. Jot down the party date, time, location and RSVP info, and mail them two weeks in advance.

COLOR SCHEME

Soften up the traditional V-Day red with a slew of pretty pinks. Whether you keep it girly with ballet pink or go bright 'n' bold with pops of bubblegum, work pink into your party supplies, food and drink. Consider asking guests to wear a specific shade of pink to theme the whole party.

DÉCOR DREAMS

From the big details (a heart-patterned tablecloth, giant LOVE letters) to the tiny ones (napkins cut into heart shapes, cupid's arrow doughnuts), this Valentine's Day is all about handmade decor. Gather glass jars and bowls of all sizes, and fill each with pink or red candy. A garland draws attention to the airy and awesome cupcake tier.

LOVE LETTERS

Spell out your heart with big block letters covered in yarn. So cute, you'll wanna keep 'em on view year-round.

[WHAT YOU'LL NEED]

Fabric wall letters in L, O, V, E (find 'em on Etsy.com) • Red yarn • Pink yarn • Scissors

[WHAT YOU'LL DO]

1. Take an end of red yarn and tie a knot around bottom of first letter.
2. Wrap knot with more yarn to cover it, continuing to fully wrap all the way around letter until you reach an approximate halfway point.
3. Leave a tail of red yarn with enough length to wrap around the letter about 4 to 5 more times, but leave it undone for now.
4. Tie a knot around the top of the letter with pink yarn, and begin to fully wrap around letter until you reach red yarn in the middle.
5. Overlap pink yarn on top of red section, allowing some red to peek through, and tuck end in. Repeat with red yarn.

SIPS AND BITES

Set a table full of sweet treats—just think pink and red. Fresh doughnuts get skewered with bamboo sticks outfitted with arrows (use a triangle of Washi tape), pink sodas get dressed up with lacy doilies and a snippet of bakers' twine, while each cupcake hides a tiny heart inside. Surprise!

Menu

Heartwarming Cupcakes*

Pink & Red Candy Bar

Cupid's Arrow Doughnuts

Natural Strawberry Soda

Find the recipe in chapter 6

ORIGAMI VALENTINES

This is a clever twist on the traditional V-Day card—small and delicate paper hearts that fit in the palm of your hand, lovingly folded by Y-O-U. Pick up a pack of printed origami paper, then mix and match. We bet everyone you love will treasure them long after February 14.

[WHAT YOU'LL NEED]

Origami paper or printed standard-weight paper • Bone folder (optional but great to have, will help you make perfect folds) • Scissors • Ruler

[WHAT YOU'LL DO]

1. Cut a piece of printed paper into a rectangle 3" wide and 6" long.
2. On a flat surface, fold rectangle in half to make a square shape.
3. Open folded rectangle and fold each of the 4 corners into center fold line. Crease folds, using bone folder if desired.
4. Leave the paper unfolded: You should have 2 X's of fold lines on each of the squares.
5. Laying paper flat horizontally in front of you, lift one side of rectangle (one square) and pinch space above and below the X lines. Bring your fingers together to fold X creases in toward center. Flatten fold to leave a layered triangle shape behind.
6. Repeat on other square. You should now have a square shape formed by 2 triangles. Rotate square so center line faces you (it becomes a diamond).
7. On one side, fold each of the triangle flaps in toward center fold. Each fold will create a mini triangle. Repeat on other side.
8. Lift one of the small triangles and open it up. Press down on tip of triangle and crease it so it meets center fold line. Repeat on 3 other triangles.
9. Turn paper over. You should have a square shape made up of 2 large triangles. Fold one triangle over on top of other, making a heart shape.
10. Turn heart over again so side with mini triangles and squares is facing up. Fold 2 corners of one square towards center line, creating a tiny kite shape. Repeat for all mini squares.
11. Turn heart over again so reverse side faces up. Fold in outer side edges of heart in towards middle, creating a flat edge instead of a point on each side.
12. Turn heart over to front side again. Lift tip of one of the kites and flatten tip down toward center, making a flat triangle at the top. Repeat for each kite.
13. You should have a pretty flower design in the middle of your heart. Flip the heart over to write a sweet note to your valentine.

Easter Egg Picnic

Honor and celebrate the resurrection of Jesus by making
your own beautiful basket of Resurrection Eggs.

Spend time with family and friends on Easter Sunday talking about
the origins of Easter: Jesus Christ's sacrifice and resurrection. After
a rousing egg hunt, gather round the (indoor) picnic blanket for a
spring feast. Bunnies optional!

SET THE SCENE

A few days prior to Easter, pick out the place inside to lay your picnic blanket. Set a small table for decorating eggs and scout outside for the best hid-
ing places to host a good old-fashioned Easter egg hunt. By the time guests
arrive, you'll have everything ready to go.

INVITE INSPIRATION

An egg-shaped card is a natural fit for Easter. Head outdoors to splatter it
with a quick coat of gold spray paint or a few flicks from a nail polish brush
and let dry. Layer a band of colored paper on top for party details, asking
guests to RSVP at least a week in advance.

COLOR SCHEME

Channel spring's greatest hits: pretty pastels in rose pink, lilac, sky blue and
mossy green with a hint of gold for good measure. Stock up on craft supplies
in these shades for the DIYs you'll be making pre-party and during the event.

DÉCOR DREAMS

Find a plaid tablecloth or a floral sheet as the spread for your Easter feast.
Lay a quilt on the carpet first for cushioning then decorate with bird cages
(find 'em at a craft store) filled with dried moss and glitzy eggs (craft
them by spray-painting cardboard egg-shaped boxes (also at a
craft store). Lay out dishes, glasses and silverware for each
guest for a very proper picnic.

FEATHER STICKS

Fluttering feathers make napkin rolls feel extra formal. Post-party, they make perfect hair sticks or fanciful additions to your pencil cup.

[WHAT YOU'LL NEED]

Bamboo skewers (1 for each napkin roll) • Scissors • Hot glue gun • Cardstock in your party's colors • Small- to medium-size feathers (found at a craft store)

[WHAT YOU'LL DO]

1. Use scissors to cut a few feather shapes (long ovals with pointed ends) from cardstock. Feathers can vary in length and width, with largest being about 2" wide and 4" tall.
2. Snip tiny cuts along perimeter of each feather to make feather's fronds, making sure not to cut all the way through.
3. Heat up hot glue gun and carefully glue a larger paper feather to end of one skewer. Layer a second smaller paper feather over top.
4. Use a dab of hot glue on top of smaller paper feather to stick on a few real feathers, spreading them out in a small fan shape.
5. Repeat for other skewers, cutting more paper feathers as needed.
6. Tuck each skewer into your rolled up napkins with silverware.

SIPS AND BITES

This spring-themed spread is all about the freshest berries you can find. Hit up your local farmer's market to test the juiciest batch. Then, use them to sweeten sparkling water or top toasted waffles. A braided Easter egg bread looks gorgeous and is simple to bake.

Menu

Easter Egg Picnic

Braided Easter Egg Bread*

Waffles with Strawberries and Cream*

Sparkling Water with Fresh Berries and Lemon

Find the recipes in chapter 6

RESURRECTION EGGS

Combining two long-lasting Easter traditions, Resurrection eggs bring the crafting fun of Easter eggs together with the history of the spring holiday. NOTE: You can either order pre-made Resurrection eggs online filled with scripture and tiny emblems of the Resurrection and decorate those, or make your own small Scripture scrolls to create your very own set.

[WHAT YOU'LL NEED]

Colorful plastic Easter eggs • Washi tape (Japanese paper tape) • Scissors

[WHAT YOU'LL DO]

1. If you're making your own, type up and print out Bible quotes (see box) onto 1 sheet of paper, then cut out each into a long strip.
2. Roll up strips of paper into tiny scrolls that you'll place inside each egg.
3. To decorate your filled eggs, cut small strips of Washi tape and apply them to each egg in a decorative pattern. Try stripes of tape, small overlapping squares, teensy triangles, crisscrossed strips or covering the entire egg. Be sure to leave opening of egg uncovered or use scissors to cut a slit through tape to read Scripture.

✳ The Resurrection Story ✳

FOLLOW THE STORY OF JESUS' RESURREC-TION THROUGH THIS SCRIPTURE

Find the passages below in the New Testament...

1. MATTHEW 21:1-3, 6-8
2. MATTHEW 26:14-16
3. MATTHEW 26:27-28
4. MARK 14:32-34
5. JOHN 19:1
6. MATTHEW 27:27-29
7. JOHN 19:16-18
8. JOHN 19:23-24
9. JOHN 19:32-34
10. MATTHEW 27:57-60
11. MATTHEW 28:2-4
12. MATTHEW 28:5-6

Christmas Cardi Party

Forget ugly sweater parties: you're having a cute cardi party!
Settle in for an afternoon of Christmas cheer while stitching
sweaters with your closest crew.

It's beginning to look a lot like Christmas: The tree is gleaming, the
stockings are hung and your best girls are coming over for a crafternoon. Ask each bud to bring a favorite cardigan to deck out, along
with a couple cold-weather items to donate to charity.

SET THE SCENE
Temporarily take over the dining room table as your new sewing space. Set
out trays of embellishments (mini sewing kits for each guest make for cute
favors) and use the sideboard or a card table as your hot cocoa bar. Hit play
on the holiday tunes before guests arrive to get in the Christmas spirit.

INVITE INSPIRATION
The holiday season is hustling and bustling, so fire off a merry evite or whip
up a red and green invitation at least three weeks in advance. Ask guests to
bring a cardigan to decorate, along with new or gently used coats, scarves,
hats and mittens for donation. Everyone can use a little extra warmth.

COLOR SCHEME
Keep things Christmas-y with a red, green and gold color scheme. Then,
decorate with abandon. Think: red napkins, a gold tablecloth, evergreens
and a gilded garland you crafted yourself.

DÉCOR DREAMS
Naturally, a fully dressed Christmas tree lends a festive atmosphere in a jiffy,
but if yours isn't up yet, start stringing the twinkle lights for instant
holiday ambience. Lay a fancy cloth over the table, break out
the tea tray for the hot cocoa bar, set out a few plates of
Christmas cookies and you're ready to fête, girl.

GILDED GARLAND

A sequin-effect garland makes any room feel suddenly sparkling.

[WHAT YOU'LL NEED]

16 metallic gold paint chips (a square shape is best; find them at a home improvement store) • Circle stencil • Xacto knife or scissors • 8' gold cord trim • Small hole punch

[WHAT YOU'LL DO]

1. Begin tracing your circle stencil onto square paint chips, cutting out circle with either an Xacto knife or scissors. No stencil? Make your own by tracing a circular object that fits area of paint chips.
2. Use hole punch to make holes about ¼" away from edge of each circle.
3. Thread gold cord through one of the paint chip holes, tying a loop around top to hold it in place.
4. Repeat for all paint chips, leaving about 6" between chips. Tape finished garland onto the edge of your hot cocoa bar, wrap it around the tree, drape it over the banister—so many options.

SIPS AND BITES

Get decadent with three flavors on your hot cocoa bar: dark, milk and white. Set out bowls of mix-ins and toppings for guests to create their own tasty concoctions. Try cinnamon sticks and candy canes for swirling, chili powder for sprinkling, marshmallows and graham crackers for topping.

Menu

Christmas Cookie Party

Hot Cocoa Trio (Dark, Milk and White)*

Cocoa Mix-in Station

Christmas Cookies

Find the recipes in chapter 6

CUTE CARDIS

Each girl should come with a cardigan in tow, but just in case someone forgot, have a few extras on hand. You can snap 'em up at the local Goodwill for cheap. Any sweaters left over? Donate them to a shelter in a bundle with any gently used scarves, hats, mittens and coats your family and friends are no longer wearing.

[WHAT YOU'LL NEED]

A cardigan that fits you well • Vintage buttons • Fabric or felt flowers • Ribbon and bows • Rhinestones and sequins • Needle and thread • Hot glue gun • Scissors

[WHAT YOU'LL DO]

1. Button up your cardigan and spread it out on a flat surface.
2. Pick out the embellishments you'd like to add to your cardigan, and decide where to place them. Don't forget sleeves or back as options, too.
3. Use needle and thread to sew embellishments in place or use hot glue gun to attach them to sweater. Try a trio of flowers along neckline or trim sleeve cuffs in bows. Need more inspo? Snip out a few pics of cute cardigans from magazines or catalogs, and remember that less here is most often more.

✳ Every day is a party ✳

A "GIVE BACK" PARTY

A charitable donation makes guests feel great, no matter the season. Ask buds to bring gently used children's books to your birthday, new school supplies to your August pool party or host a canned food drive at Thanksgiving. There are a million ways to help others while having fun. Choose your favorite cause and get giving.

SOIRÉE SECRETS

From how to pull off a perfect surprise party to solving those bash blunders, we're getting into the nitty gritty of party planning.

THROW A SUCCESSFUL SURPRISE PARTY

So you want to conquer the surprise soirée? Here's your cheat sheet to mastering the art of the sneak attack.

PLAN IT: A surprise birthday party calls for major advance planning. You'll need to loop in key people (the guest of honor's parents and closest crew) about a month ahead of your girl's birthday to make sure you're picking a date where she has no other engagements. If it's on her actual birthday, have someone make faux plans so she doesn't get suspicious.

PICK THE PLACE: Once your date has been decided, set your sights on the location. Having a party at your house might be easiest—you can invite her over without her thinking twice, but it's also fun to transform her own abode into a surprise setup. Or, have a hangout at the ice skating rink or her go-to Thai place. Just make sure you've got the girl of the hour's favorite interests in mind.

GET THE WORD OUT: Got the where and when? Send out party invites to your guest list at least three weeks in advance. Ask guests to arrive one hour before the birthday girl to make sure everyone's there for the actual surprise. Don't forget to write on the invitation that the party's a secret—you don't want to tell You Know Who about her own surprise party. Shh!

DISTRACT HER: You'll need to be extra sneaky for this step. Make different plans with the birthday girl and a couple friends to make sure she has no idea what's actually up. Maybe they'll take her to the mall for a quick shopping trip while you get the party prepped, or treat her to her fave hot cocoa at the corner café. Have your friends text you when they've got her in tow and are headed to the party location, about 30 minutes after everyone else has already arrived.

PLAN OUT EVERYTHING: We're betting she can recognize the cars of all her friends, so tell moms to do drop offs around the block. And remind everyone to nix any social media chatter—any wisp of a party mention and she's bound to clue in. And try not to spoil the surprise yourself—seeing her smiling face when it actually happens is totally worth the wait.

SET UP THE FINAL SNEAK ATTACK: Ten minutes before the birthday girl's arrival, shut off the lights and hide everyone behind furniture. Instruct all the guests that when she walks in and you flip the light switch, they should jump out, toss some confetti and scream, "Surprise!" Have a couple people ready to shoot pics and video. The look on her face? Priceless.

BASH BLUNDERS

We know you'll do your best to make sure everything is going smoothly, but even the best parties don't always go as planned and, sometimes, somebody just wants to sulk. Here's how to get your bash back on track...

PARTY PROB: NO ONE'S TALKING. Sounds like it's time for an instant ice-breaker. A crowd fave is the game "Truth or Lie": Go first and tell two truths and one falsehood about yourself. Give everyone a chance to guess which statement is a lie before revealing the answer, then designate the next storyteller.

PARTY PROB: PEOPLE AREN'T PARTICIPATING. Coax your guests to take part by suggesting that sitting out means they're missing out on a lot of fun. If they're persistent, let them be and continue to have fun with your other buds—don't let one person's sour mood ruin your party.

PARTY PROB: SOMEONE'S HOMESICK. Your pal's got the blues and just wants to head home? Smile, give her a hug and thank her for coming. A good hostess is always understanding—if she really wants to leave, let her go.

PARTY PROB: THINGS ARE GETTING A LI'L CRAZY. The party temperature is rising a bit too high? Regain control by turning the music down a couple levels

ops!
ummy bear
rty foul.

or suggesting a different (quieter) activity. That's not working? It's time to call in reinforcements. Mom or Dad can help calm things down, stat.

FRIEND OR FOE?

Sometimes even a close bud can turn the best bash into a bummer. Here's how to handle any pesky party personalities…

UNSATISFIED SISTAH

For her, nothing's ever quite up to snuff…from the sodas not being cold enough to the games not being fun enough, she'd rather sit out and gripe than actually try to have a good time—and she'll make sure you know it.

HANDLE IT: Truth is, some people just wanna whine. Try to shrug off her rude remarks without getting frosty. The Sprite is a little warm? Steer her toward the ice. She thinks Crush, Kiss, BF is a drag? A simple, "We're all having a blast!" will remind this chica that she's the one keeping herself from enjoying the good time. Don't let one girl bring the party down.

3 FUN PARTY GAMES

1. ANIMAL CHARADES. The classic party game, with a twist. Divide into two teams and have each team write down a list of animals on strips of paper for the opposite team to act out. Place the strips into a hat for each team, then have one team member pick a strip and act out the animal, using only hand motions and sounds. No talking!

2. KNEES UP. Pair up party members and ask them to sit down back to back and link arms. Then, each pair has to try to stand up while keeping backs touching and elbows linked. First pair standing wins. Dare ya not to bust up laughing.

3. TELEPHONE. Sit the group in a circle, then whisper a silly phrase to the person on your right. That person whispers the phrase to the person on her right, and so on, until the phrase gets back to you. We bet you'll hardly recognize it!

PARTY PIRATE

Sure, it's your party, but the Party Pirate still wants to be the center of attention. From stealing the show at karaoke to photo-bombing all the snapshots, she has literally plundered your party.

HANDLE IT: Don't make her walk the plank. Switch gears with an activity that'll give everyone a chance to shine. Start up a game of charades and let her pick the teams to make her feel important, then get the rest of the group involved in the game. Hopefully, this pirate will pipe down. Come her turn, she'll have to!

WALLOWING WALLFLOWER

She's the one who hasn't budged from the snack table since she showed up. You barely got her to take off her coat. When you turned up the volume on your fave track, everyone started dancing—but not her. You've tried to include her in the party craft, to no avail. What gives?

HANDLE IT: There's a shy girl at every party, and it's your job as hostess to help her get out of her shell. Rather than pawning her off on another pal, enlist her to help you with hostess duties. She can lend a hand as you refill drinks and tidy up the kitchen, then get her talking. A little one-on-one time just might open her up.

BE THE BEST GUEST

Wanna wow the pants off the party planner? Here are seven ways to make sure you're on your very best guest behavior.

RSVP ASAP

Imagine trying to host a party with absolutely no idea how many guests will be attending. It's every hostess' worst nightmare! Soothe her fears by returning your RSVP promptly (as in, long before the deadline). She'll be ever so grateful.

TOTE A TRINKET

Bringing a little gift to your hostess' house is a small gesture of sweetness that definitely won't go unnoticed. And your present doesn't have to cost a pretty penny: Consider whipping up a batch of your fave brownies, picking out a bouquet of blooms from the farmer's market or wrapping up a cute set of stationery. We guarantee you'll get invited back.

PRACTICE PUNCTUALITY

Truth: There's really no such thing as being "fashionably late." You're just plain late. Besides, walking in the door past the party's start time might mean you'll be missing out on game rules, cake cutting or other fun surprises. On the other

Checklist

Pleasing the parental units

Having Mom and Dad around to help out during your party isn't a bad thing—you'll want their assistance in case anything goes awry. But we get that you'll want your space, too. Circle up pre-party to make sure everyone's on the same page...

❑ **Plan out the party flow:** Let them know when you'll be doing what so they won't have to hover.

❑ **Review the house rules:** Clarify which rooms are off-limits and whether you can go outside after dark.

❑ **Give the 'rents a task:** Maybe Mom can help with the decorations and Dad can grill the burgers, but after those jobs are done, ask for a little privacy.

❑ **Work out the sibling sitch:** If your sis always wants to shadow you, ask Mom if she can play at a friend's house. Big bro hogs the TV every Friday night? Nicely ask if he can record the game to watch it later.

❑ **Be considerate:** Remember, your family lives here, too! Willingness to compromise and abide by their rules just might guarantee your happy future of party hostessing.

❑ **Be gracious:** A little thank-you goes a long way. Post-party, tuck a note into Dad's briefcase or send Mom a short email saying how grateful you were to have a party, and how much fun you had!

hand, show up too early and you'll unintentionally hassle a frazzled hostess. Sure, you can offer up your services, but it's best to just arrive on time.

PARENT PROCEDURES

Trust us, everybody has felt homesick at a party at least once. If it's happening to you, here's how to deal: Discreetly ask the host if you can use her phone, or tell her you'll quickly step outside to call your parents on your cell. Tell Mom or Dad how you're feeling, and they can assess whether to pick you up to leave the party early. Sometimes, just hearing a parent's voice on the other end might quell your qualms. Other times, a girl just needs to go home. And that's A-OK!

MAKING AN EXIT

Whether you've got a prior engagement or are coming down with a case of the homesick blues, leaving early from a party isn't a crime—you just have to handle it the right way. If possible, notify your hostess a few days before the party that you'll be leaving early, and remind her again when you arrive. When the time comes, make a swift exit, saying a short 'n' sweet sayonara to your hostess and the other guests without taking too much attention away from the party's goings-on.

OVERNIGHTS: WHAT TO PACK

Headed to your first slumber party? Be sure to stash the following items in your overnight bag:

- Pillow
- Sleeping bag
- Pajamas
- Toothbrush and toothpaste
- Change of clothes for the next morning
- Any activities you may want to bring: your fave new nail polish, a game you love, a movie you want to watch
- A gift for the birthday girl, if necessary

THANK HER KINDLY

Had a blast at your bestie's bash? Let her know with a quick thank-you note or send off a sweet email. Be sure to include how glad you were to be invited, how much fun you had and how much you loved doing one of the specific activities she had planned. Thank her again, and be sure to invite her to your next party to return the favor!

GOODNIGHTS AND GOODBYES

Whether it's lights out at your sleepover or Mom has threatened to turn you into a pumpkin if your pals haven't vanished by 8pm, goodnights and good-byes don't have to be sad affairs.

SLEEP TIGHT

Keep in mind that different girls have different bedtimes—and it's kinda rude not to let someone hit the hay when they want. When it gets to the wee hours, play a quiet game so early birds can catch some zzzs while night owls stay up late.

CIAO FOR NOW

Time to leave? Help your friends gather their belongings and walk each girl to the door. Sweetly thank them for coming to your party and send them on their way. Once all the partygoers are gone, help Mom and Dad tidy things up.

GOOD 'N' GRACIOUS

It seems a tad stuffy and a bit formal, but the proper way to thank a guest for bringing a gift to your bash is still by mailing her a handwritten thank-you note. You have about a week after the party to get them out, so start scribblin', sweetie!

CLEAN SWEEP

Party's over, but who's gonna take care of this mess? Enlist a few friends (or your sibs) to help you straighten up. Recycle any stray cups, put away the leftover snacks, load the dishwasher, move the furniture back and take down the décor. You can even give out your garlands and streamers as cleaning crew favors.

Every day is a party

From checking off your checklists (twice!) to mastering the party flow to battling bash blunders and commandeering the cleanup crew, dare we say you're becoming a pretty fabulous hostess. But why stop there? Here are four more awesome ways to make EVERY day a party…

❑ Dish it up. Celebrate life's smallest occasions. Whether it's making a smoothie after a great hike with Dad or whipping up baby bro's fave muffins after his T-ball team makes the finals, you'll be amazed at how a little effort can make any day— and anyone—suddenly feel extra special.

❑ Dial it up. Nothing makes a party (or a Wednesday!) feel more festive than putting on a fun playlist. Dance competition in the living room? You bet.

❑ Turn it on. Next Friday night, make it a movie marathon with a slew of cheesy '80s movies, some funny rom-coms or even your old favorite cartoons. Settle in with some popcorn and bust out the fuzzy slippers.

❑ Break it out. You know that puzzle you never finished? The knitting project you took up but put down last Christmas? Break out the supplies, rope in your pals and have a blast bonding over the activities you're all normally too busy for. Watch the fun unfold: Suddenly, you're having a party!

RECIPES

Really want to show your guests you care? Just one homemade sip or bite is all you need to make your party that much more memorable. Dial up the heartfelt details with simple trailmix popcorn balls for movie night or made-from-scratch waffles for your next sleepover. So much more special than tearing open that bag of chips, right?

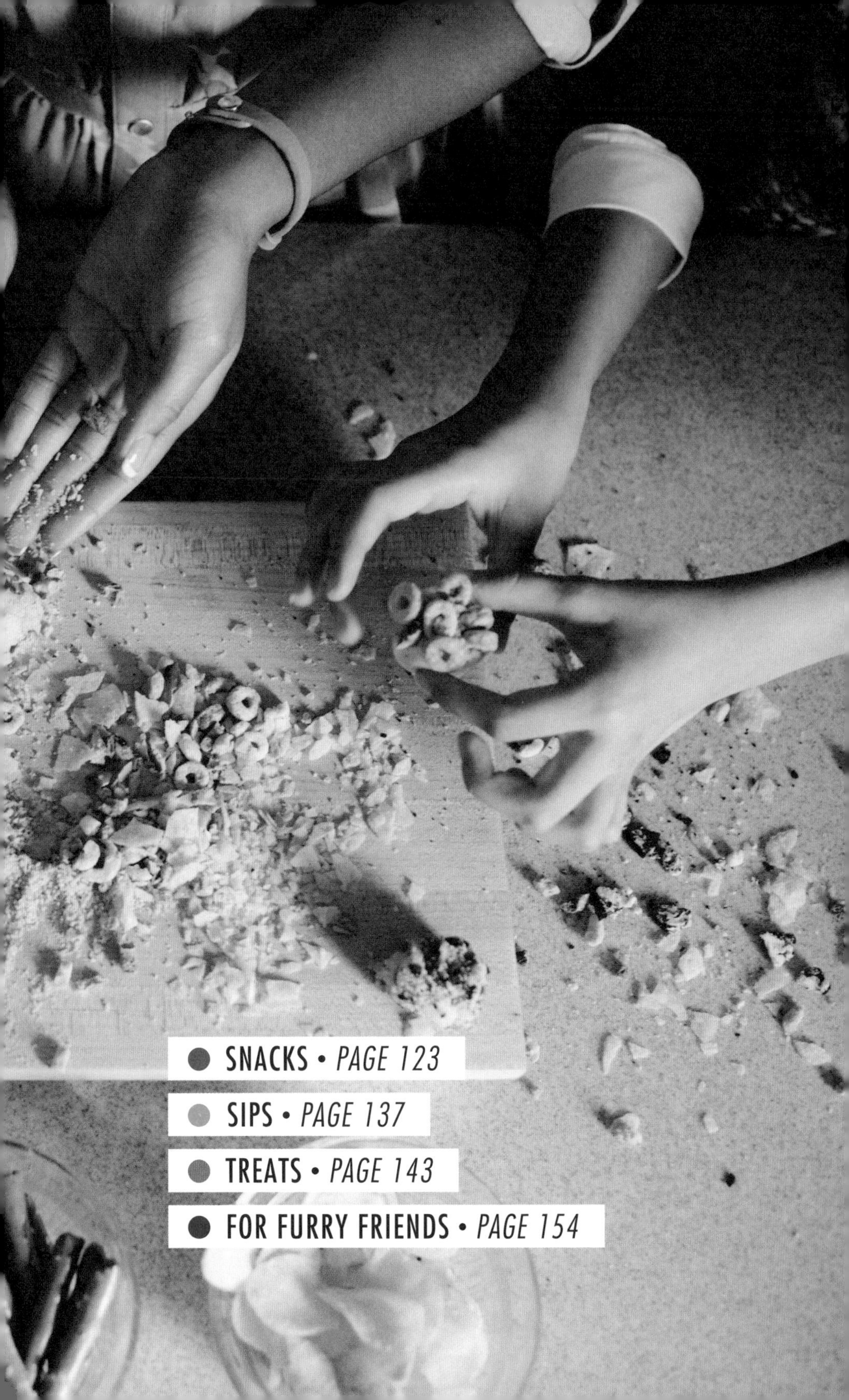

SNACKS

TRIPLE BERRY LEMON MUFFINS

CUCUMBER CREAM CHEESE ROUNDS

CHEESY FONDUE AND DIPPERS

WAFFLES WITH STRAWBERRIES & CREAM

TRAILMIX POPCORN BALLS

BRAIDED EASTER EGG BREAD

POPCORN SEASONING SPICES

FRUITY COCONUT WATER POPSICLES

SWEET AND SPICY CANDIED NUTS

SIPS

HOT COCOA TRIO

MINT LEMONADE

SWEET MANGO MINT SMOOTHIE

ROOT BEER FLOAT

ROSEWATER ICED TEA

TREATS

CHOCOLATE FONDUE AND DIPPERS

SPRINKLE SURPRISE CAKE

PUFFY PINK MARSHMALLOWS

HEARTWARMING CUPCAKES

STAR-SHAPED COOKIE BARS

PINK CHOCOLATE DIPPED WAFFLE CONES

SALTED CARAMEL BROWNIES

FOR FURRY FRIENDS

BONE UP DOG BISCUITS

STARFISH CAT TREATS

● TRIPLE BERRY LEMON MUFFINS ●

These lemony berry muffins make for perfect brunch fare.
Topped with a dollop of yogurt, they're also a healthy and
delicious quick breakfast!

MAKES 12 MUFFINS

1 ½ cups flour

1 cup sugar

1 teaspoon salt

2 teaspoons baking powder

⅓ cup butter, melted

1 egg

⅓ cup milk

2 teaspoons vanilla extract

½ cup raspberries

½ cup blueberries

½ cup strawberries

1 teaspoon lemon extract

FOR THE CRUMB TOPPING:

⅓ cup brown sugar

⅓ cup flour

¼ cup butter, softened

1 teaspoon cinnamon

1. Preheat oven to 400°F. Line a 12 cup muffin tin with paper liners.

2. In a medium bowl, mix flour, sugar, salt and baking powder. Set aside.

3. In a small bowl, stir together butter, egg, milk and vanilla.

4. Fold egg mixture into flour mixture, stirring until just combined.

5. Gently fold in berries and lemon extract.

6. Fill each muffin cup ⅔ of the way with batter.

7. In a separate bowl, create the crumb topping. Cut together the brown sugar, flour, butter and cinnamon until the mixture resembles coarse meal. Top each muffin with crumbs.

8. Bake muffins for 20 to 25 minutes, or until golden brown.

● CUCUMBER CREAM CHEESE ROUNDS ●

These delightful savory sandwiches are almost too cute to eat! Almost.

MAKES ABOUT 30 ROUNDS

1 loaf sliced white bread

2 large English cucumbers

8 oz. cream cheese, softened

2 tablespoons fresh chives, chopped, plus more for garnish

1. Use a round cookie cutter to cut out about 30 rounds of white bread, making sure to skip crust. The circumference of your cookie cutter should generally match that of your cucumbers.

2. Thinly slice cucumbers into about ¼" thick rounds.

3. In a small bowl, use a spatula to mix cream cheese with chives.

4. Spread a bread round with a swipe of cream cheese mixture, then top with a cucumber. Top with a tiny dollop of cream cheese and garnish with a sliver of chive. Repeat for all bread rounds.

● CHEESY FONDUE AND DIPPERS ●

This tasty cheese creation will certainly take center stage at your next event. Cut up all dippers (except apples) a couple hours ahead of serving and refrigerate until ready to serve.

SERVES 8 to 10

½ pound Swiss or Emmentaler cheese

½ pound Gruyere cheese

2 cloves garlic

3 tablespoons flour

2 tablespoons butter

1 ½ cups milk

⅛ teaspoon nutmeg

Salt and pepper

½ teaspoon lemon juice

DIPPERS:

Cubed pieces of baguette and/or pumpernickel bread

Broccoli florets

Red bell pepper slices

Celery sticks

Baby carrots

Apple wedges

1. Before you start making the fondue, have all dippers cut and arranged on a tray so they're ready to go.

2. Peel garlic and cut in half lengthwise. Rub a saucepan with two garlic halves, and rub inside of fondue pot with remaining halves.

3. Grate cheeses and mix with 1 tablespoon flour.

4. Melt butter in saucepan over medium-low heat. Add remaining flour, stirring until smooth.

5. Slowly add milk in ½ cup increments, stirring constantly until mixture thickens.

6. Add in a handful of cheese, stirring until cheese is melted. Continue adding cheese, a handful at a time, stirring until all the cheese is melted.

7. Stir in nutmeg and season with salt and pepper. Add lemon juice, stirring well.

8. Light tealight under your fondue pot and serve.

● WAFFLES WITH STRAWBERRIES & CREAM ●

There's nothing better than waking up to waffles in the morning.
Serve these up at your next sleepover or picnic party. No waffle iron?
You can use this batter to make pancakes, too.

6 to 8 WAFFLES

3 tablespoons butter, melted

1 ½ cups flour

1 ½ teaspoons baking powder

¼ teaspoon salt

2 tablespoons sugar

1 ½ cups whole milk

2 eggs

½ teaspoon vanilla extract

FOR TOPPING:

1 cup washed and sliced strawberries

Whipped cream

1. Preheat waffle iron while you melt butter in microwave.

2. In a large mixing bowl, combine flour, baking powder, salt and sugar.

3. In a small bowl, whisk together milk, eggs and vanilla.

4. Whisk together wet and dry ingredients until just combined, then stir in melted butter.

5. Spray waffle iron with nonstick cooking spray, and use spoon to drop ½ cup of batter onto iron. Close to cook, watching until edges of waffle turn golden brown.

6. Place waffle on plate and keep hot in warming oven. Repeat step 5 for rest of batter.

7. Once all waffles are cooked, top each with dollop of whipped cream and several slices of strawberries.

SNACKS

● TRAILMIX POPCORN BALLS ●

Partly sweet and partly salty, these chewy popcorn balls are all delicious. Add in your own favorite trailmix ingredients!

MAKES ABOUT 24 POPCORN BALLS

12 cups popped popcorn

1 cup sugar

⅓ cup light corn syrup

⅓ cup water

1 teaspoon distilled white vinegar

1 teaspoon sea salt

¼ cup butter

1 cup peanuts

1 cup M&M candies

1 cup raisins

1. Pour popcorn into a large soup pot or your largest heatproof bowl. Set aside.

2. Combine sugar, corn syrup, water, vinegar and salt in a small saucepan. Stir over high heat until sugar is dissolved. Bring to a boil and cook 5 to 7 minutes, or until temperature reaches 260°F on a candy thermometer. Remove from heat and stir in butter until melted. No thermometer? Carefully drop a spoonful of the sugar mixture into a bowl of very cold water. Use your hand to form the sugar mixture into a ball underwater. When removed from the water, ball should hold its shape but remain sticky.

3. Drizzle ⅓ of sugar mixture over popcorn and stir with a rubber spatula until popcorn is coated, adding another ⅓ of sugar mixture. Before you add in last ⅓, add peanuts, M&Ms and raisins, then pour in rest of sugar mixture.

4. Grease hands with butter and press mixture into 3" balls. Place balls on cookie sheet to cool. Serve on a platter or wrap each in cellophane to make fun favors.

● BRAIDED EASTER EGG BREAD ●

Prepare to be dazzled: This fluffy golden bread is deliciously scented with lemon—and looks quite impressive to boot.

SERVES 6 to 8

¼ cup sugar

1 teaspoon salt

1 package active dry yeast

3 ½ cups flour, divided

2 tablespoons butter

⅔ cup milk

6 eggs

2 teaspoons lemon extract

1 teaspoon vanilla extract

Easter-egg coloring kit

1 teaspoon water

1. About 5 hours before serving, mix sugar, salt, yeast and 1 cup flour in bowl.

2. Heat butter and milk in microwave until very warm (125°F).

3. With stand mixer at low speed, beat liquid ingredients into dry ingredients.

4. Turn speed to medium, then beat in 2 eggs and 1 egg white (reserve yolk), along with ¾ cup flour. Mix in extracts and 1 ¼ cups flour.

5. Turn out dough onto floured surface and coat palms in flour. Use hands to knead dough for 5 minutes, working in ½ cup flour.

6. Place dough in a greased bowl, turning dough to grease all sides. Cover bowl with plastic wrap and a clean, dry dishtowel. Let dough rise in a warm place until doubled, or for about 1 ½ hours.

7. Meanwhile, dye 3 eggs using Easter-egg coloring kit, but do not hard-boil eggs. Set aside once dyed.

8. After dough has risen, punch down dough and turn out onto a floured surface. Cover and let rise again for 15 minutes.

9. Grease a large cookie sheet. Cut dough in half and mold each half into a 30" long rope. Place both ropes on cookie sheet, twist together to join and attach ends to form a circle. Cover and let rise until doubled, or for 1 ½ hours.

10. Preheat the oven to 350°F. Gently press 3 dyed eggs into twists.

11. In a small bowl, beat reserved egg yolk with 1 teaspoon water and brush mixture over top of dough.

12. Bake dough 30 minutes or until golden brown. Let cool on wire rack before serving. When serving, remove eggs—don't eat them, they may not be fully cooked.

SNACKS

● POPCORN SEASONING SPICES ●

What's your flavor? Whether it's salty or sweet, chocolaty or spicy, we've got the popcorn topping mix for you.

MAKES 4 4 OZ. JARS

COOL RANCH SEASONING:

1 tablespoon buttermilk powder (found in the baking section)

1 tablespoon dried dill

1 tablespoon onion salt

1 tablespoon garlic powder

COCOA CHILI POWDER SEASONING:

1 tablespoon unsweetened cocoa powder

2 tablespoons sugar

½ tablespoon chili powder

CINNAMON SUGAR SEASONING:

1 tablespoon cinnamon

2 tablespoons brown sugar

CHOCOLATY RAISIN SPRINKLES SEASONING:

2 tablespoons rainbow sprinkles

2 tablespoons chocolate-covered raisins

1. Choose your seasoning mixture and add all ingredients to a 4 oz. glass jar with a lid (any jar will do!).

2. Screw on lid tightly and shake to combine.

3. Use a spoon to sprinkle over hot buttered popcorn and serve.

SNACKS

● FRUITY COCONUT WATER POPSICLES ●

There's nothing more refreshing than a popsicle on a hot summer day. The list of fruits below is our fave combo, but use whatever you have on hand.

SERVES 6 to 8

Coconut water (found at
a health food store)

Orange slices

Kiwi slices

Pomegranate seeds

Raspberries

Blueberries

1. Fill popsicle molds with fruit and berries.

2. Pour coconut water over top to fill, being careful not to overfill molds.

3. Freeze for at least 2 hours, then enjoy. To release popsicles, run warm water over outside of the mold until popsicle loosens.

SNACKS

● SWEET AND SPICY CANDIED NUTS ●

These toasty, tangy morsels are sure to curb cravings.

MAKES 2 CUPS

2 tablespoons unsalted butter

2 tablespoons brown sugar

2 tablespoons water

½ teaspoon sea salt

½ cup almonds

½ cup cashews

½ cup peanuts

½ cup pecans

½ teaspoon chili powder

½ teaspoon cinnamon

¼ teaspoon nutmeg

½ teaspoon rosemary

1. Line a baking sheet with parchment paper and set aside.

2. In a large skillet over medium heat, melt butter and add sugar and water.

3. Add salt, almonds, cashews, peanuts and pecans, chili powder, cinnamon and nutmeg.

4. Stir and cook until butter is melted, nuts are fragrant and water has mostly evaporated, or about 8 minutes.

5. Add rosemary and stir. Spread nut mixture onto prepared baking sheet to cool completely before serving.

● HOT COCOA TRIO ●

With three flavors to choose from, just one mug is never enough.

SERVES 4

MILK CHOCOLATE COCOA

4 cups milk

10 oz. milk chocolate chips

1 teaspoon vanilla extract

DARK CHOCOLATE COCOA

4 cups milk

10 oz. semi-sweet chocolate chips

1 teaspoon vanilla extract

WHITE CHOCOLATE COCOA

4 cups milk

10 oz. white chocolate chips

1 teaspoon vanilla extract

1. Choose the cocoa flavor you'll be making, then use microwave to heat milk in a glass vessel or microwave-safe bowl to nearly boiling.

2. Stir in chocolate chips and vanilla until frothy and chocolate is melted.

3. Serve immediately with your favorite toppings from the hot cocoa bar. (We heart candy canes, cinnamon sticks, graham cracker pieces and marshmallows.)

● **MINT LEMONADE** ●

This lemonade seems to quench thirst even better when combined with fresh mint. Ahhh.

SERVES 8

6 cups water

2 cups sugar

2 cups fresh-squeezed lemon juice (you'll need to juice about 12 lemons with a hand juicer)

½ cup fresh mint leaves

1. Bring 2 cups water and sugar to a boil in a small saucepan over high heat, stirring occasionally.

2. Lower heat and simmer until mixture is transparent, about 5 minutes.

3. Remove from heat and let cool to room temperature.

4. In large pitcher, add lemon juice, 4 cups water and 1 cup of sugar syrup. Stir in mint leaves.

5. Refrigerate 1 hour and serve over ice.

● SWEET MANGO MINT SMOOTHIE ●

There's something so transporting about whipping up a smoothie with tropical flavors. Make it whenever you need a quick vacay.

2 12 OZ. SMOOTHIES

1 ½ cups mango

1 cup coconut milk (found at a health food store)

2 teaspoons agave nectar or honey (or more to taste)

Handful of ice cubes

3 mint leaves plus garnish

1. Add all ingredients to blender and blend on high speed until combined.

2. Pour into a tall glass and garnish with an extra mint leaf or two.

● ROOT BEER FLOAT ●

Why not drink your dessert? The classic root beer float is unparalleled.

2 12 OZ. FLOATS

Vanilla ice cream

16 oz. root beer

1. Add 2 scoops of vanilla ice cream to a tall glass.

2. Slowly pour root beer over ice cream, allowing it to foam up and recede before pouring more root beer.

3. Stick in a straw and serve with a spoon. Want to change it up? Pour seltzer over lime sherbet, or cherry soda over vanilla ice cream, and make it extra festive with whipped cream and sprinkles.

● **ROSEWATER ICED TEA** ●

Sweetly floral, this iced tea will become your go-to
summer cool-down drink.

SERVES 8

6 cups water

2 cups sugar

2 tablespoons rosewater
(found at a health food store)

2 bags of caffeine-free
black tea

Ice

1. Bring 2 cups water and the sugar to a boil in a small saucepan over high heat, stirring occasionally.

2. Lower heat and simmer until mixture is transparent, about 5 minutes.

3. Remove from heat and let cool to room temperature. Stir in rosewater.

4. Fill another saucepan with 2 cups of water and bring to a boil. In the meantime, tie strings of teabags to handle of a wooden spoon. When water boils, turn off heat and add tea bags, laying spoon across the rim of pot, and let steep for 5 minutes.

5. Pour tea into large pitcher, adding 2 cups cold water and ice to fill. Sweeten with rosewater syrup, adding 2 tablespoons at a time to taste. Stir and refrigerate for 1 hour. Serve over ice.

TREATS

● CHOCOLATE FONDUE AND DIPPERS ●

Is there anything more decadent than dipping fruit and sweets
into warm melted chocolate? We think not.

SERVES 8 to 10

12 oz. dark chocolate
½ pint whipping cream

DIPPERS:
Strawberries
Banana coins
Apple wedges
Mini chocolate chip cookies
Pound cake cubes
Marshmallows

1. Before you start making the fondue, have all dippers cut and arranged on a tray so they're ready to go.

2. Place chocolate in small saucepan over low heat and stir until melted.

3. Slowly add in whipping cream, stirring until mixture is smooth.

4. Pour chocolate fondue into fondue pot, lighting tealight underneath. No fondue pot? Make this minutes before serving and tell friends to eat fast. Shouldn't be a problem!

● SPRINKLE SURPRISE CAKE ●

Imagine the surprise on a birthday girl's face when you present her with this rainbow sprinkle-covered cake.

MAKES 1 2 LAYERED 9" ROUND CAKE

½ cup butter, softened, plus 1-2 tablespoons more for the pan

1 ½ cups sugar

3 eggs

2 ¼ cups flour

Scant (just barely) teaspoon salt

3 ½ teaspoons baking powder

1 ¼ cups 2% milk

2 teaspoons vanilla extract

FOR THE FROSTING:

2 cups powdered sugar

½ cup or 1 stick butter, softened

1 teaspoon vanilla extract

2 tablespoons 2% milk

16 oz rainbow sprinkles

1. Preheat oven to 350°F while you butter 2 9"-round cake pans. Sprinkle flour over them, shake to cover evenly and tap out excess. Set aside.

2. Use stand mixer or hand mixer to cream the butter and sugar together until fluffy. Add eggs one at a time, beating on medium low speed.

3. Add flour, salt, baking powder and milk and vanilla, beating until fully combined. Turn speed up to medium high and beat for 3 minutes.

4. Pour batter into prepared pans and bake 25 to 30 minutes, or until top is golden brown and a toothpick inserted in center comes out clean.

5. While cake bakes, prepare frosting: Beat all ingredients in medium bowl until smooth and no lumps remain. If mixture is too dry or clumpy, add a touch more milk.

6. Let cakes cool for 15 minutes, then flip one pan over onto cutting board and lightly tap bottom of pan with blunt edge of butter knife. Cake should release from pan onto cutting board, but if not, let it cool longer. Repeat for second cake.

7. Place one cake right side up on cake stand or dinner plate. Spread on thin layer of frosting, then place second cake directly on top of first.

8. Cover entire cake surface with frosting.

9. Coat cake entirely in sprinkles, using hands to press them onto the sides of cake if necessary.

● PUFFY PINK MARSHMALLOWS ●

Pillow soft and pink(!), these marshmallows will ruin you for store-bought ones maybe forever. Grab Mom's help for this recipe. Short on time? You can find gourmet marshmallows at a specialty food store.

....

MAKES ABOUT 100 MARSHMALLOWS
....

½ cup powdered sugar

1 oz. or 4 packets unflavored gelatin powder

⅓ cup + ½ cup water, divided

2 cups sugar

½ cup light corn syrup

3 egg whites

2 tablespoons vanilla extract

Scant (just barely) ¼ teaspoon cream of tartar

¼ teaspoon salt

5 drops red food coloring

1. Coat 9" x 13" cake pan with cooking spray. Sprinkle powdered sugar mixture into pan, tapping sides to evenly coat pan's surface, and pour excess into small bowl, reserving for later.

2. Add gelatin to different small bowl. Pour ⅓ cup water on top of gelatin, lightly swirl with metal spoon and set aside to harden.

3. In small saucepan, add ½ cup water, sugar and corn syrup. Stir with spatula over medium low heat. Use candy thermometer to heat mixture to 230°F over about 12 minutes.

4. Set up stand mixer with whisk attachment, then add egg whites, vanilla, cream of tartar and salt to bowl.

5. Once sugar mixture on stove reaches 230°F, begin beating egg white mixture.

6. Keep heating sugar mixture on stove. When sugar mixture hits 246°F (about 3 more minutes), remove pan from heat and whisk in gelatin until fully combined, moving quickly.

7. Keep mixer running and add hot sugar/gelatin mixture into egg mixture at a very slow stream. Then, increase mixer speed to medium high. Continue mixing until soft peaks that hold their shape have begun to form.

8. Fold in red food coloring, stirring with rubber spatula until mixture is pink.

9. Use spatula to push mixture into prepared pan. Cover with plastic wrap and chill for at least 3 hours until fully set.

10. Once set, sprinkle sugar on top of marshmallow, spreading to cover. Cut 1" squares and roll each square in powdered sugar until all sides are covered. Shake off excess. Store marshmallows in an air-tight container for up to a week.

● HEARTWARMING CUPCAKES ●

A bitty heart-shaped cookie cutter is all you need to sneak
a heartfelt surprise inside these yummy cupcakes.

MAKES 12 CUPCAKES

2 cups flour

1 ½ cups sugar

3 ½ teaspoons baking powder

1 teaspoon salt

½ cup butter, plus more for the pan

1 cup whole milk

1 teaspoon vanilla

4 egg whites

Red food coloring

1. Heat oven to 350°F. Butter and flour a 9" square baking pan. Fill a muffin tin with cupcake liners.

2. Sift together flour, sugar, baking powder and salt. Stir and set aside.

3. Using stand mixer, beat dry ingredients along with butter, ⅔ cup of the milk and vanilla on low speed for 30 seconds. Use spatula to scrape down sides of bowl.

4. Turn speed to high and beat mixture for 2 minutes.

5. Add rest of the milk and egg whites. Beat on high for 2 minutes.

6. Separate out approximately 1 ½ cups of batter into a separate small bowl. Stir in 8 drops of red food coloring. Presto, now it's pink!

7. Pour pink batter into prepared 9" square pan and bake for 12 to 14 minutes. Do not overbake.

8. Let pink cake cool for 5 minutes, then use small heart-shaped cookie cutter (about 1" wide) to cut out 12 heart shapes to place inside the full cupcakes. Discard scraps.

9. Fill each muffin cup with a dollop of the white batter, then place one heart standing up inside cup. Fill cup with batter until heart is just covered. Repeat for all muffin cups.

10. Bake for 20 minutes uncovered, then cover with foil and bake for another 10 minutes.

11. Let cupcakes cool completely before icing.

● STAR-SHAPED COOKIE BARS ●

This recipe is infinitely adaptable. Swap the chocolate chips for mini peanut butter cups, chocolate covered raisins or nuts.

MAKES 12 to 16 STARS, DEPENDING ON SIZE OF CUTTER

1 cup or 2 sticks melted butter, plus 1-2 tablespoons more for the pan

2 ½ cups flour

1 teaspoon baking powder

½ teaspoon salt

1 ½ cups packed brown sugar

2 eggs

2 teaspoons vanilla extract

½ cup semi-sweet chocolate chips

1. Preheat oven to 350°F. Butter a 9" square baking pan. Line pan with parchment, leaving an overhang on two sides, then butter the parchment.

2. Sift together flour, baking powder and salt, whisk and then set aside.

3. In large bowl, whisk together butter, brown sugar, eggs and vanilla until smooth. Add flour mixture and stir until just combined, being sure not to overmix. Fold in chocolate chips.

4. Spread batter in prepared pan and bake 40 to 45 minutes, or until toothpick inserted in the center comes out clean. Let cool 15 minutes in the pan, then lift parchment paper edges to raise cookie bars out of pan.

5. Use varying sizes of star-shaped cookie cutters to cut stars out of cookie bars while still warm. Be careful, as metal cutters can transfer heat from cookie and become very hot. Discard scraps and let stars cool completely.

● PINK CHOCOLATE-DIPPED WAFFLE CONES ●

Dare to get darling: Swirled waffle cones in pink
chocolate complete with a double scoop of ice cream,
please! Don't forget the sprinkles.

MAKES 12 CONES

12 waffle cones

11 oz. bag white
chocolate chips

Red food coloring

1. Remove cones from box and stand 3 cones
upright in 4 shallow glasses or jars.

2. In microwave-safe bowl, melt white chocolate
chips in 10 second increments, stirring every
time until mixture is smooth.

3. Stir in 20 to 25 drops of red food coloring, or until desired color is reached.

4. Roll opening of one cone into chocolate mixture, swirling to cover 1" on
outside rim. Stand cone upright in glass or jar so it doesn't touch tops of other
cones. Repeat for all cones, letting chocolate set until hardened.

● SALTED CARAMEL BROWNIES ●

A swirl of caramel and a sprinkling of sea salt makes
these fudgy brownies super gourmet.

MAKES 1 9"X13" PAN OF BROWNIES

1 cup or 2 sticks butter,
plus 1 to 2 tablespoons more
for the pan

1 cup flour

2 cups sugar

Scant (just barely) ½
teaspoon salt

4 oz. dark baking chocolate
(we like Baker's brand,
found in the baking section
at the grocery store)

4 eggs

1½ teaspoons vanilla
extract

¼ cup caramel sauce
(store-bought is OK!)

1½ teaspoons coarse sea salt

1. Preheat oven to 350°F. Butter a 9" x 13"
baking pan.

2. Combine flour, sugar and salt in a small bowl,
set aside.

3. Melt chocolate and butter in a small saucepan
over low heat, stirring constantly.

4. Remove mixture from heat and stir in the
sugar. Allow to cool slightly.

5. Beat in eggs one at a time, then stir in vanilla.

6. Incorporate dry ingredients into wet, until just
combined.

7. Pour batter into prepared pan. Drizzle caramel
sauce over top of batter, then use a butter knife to
lightly swirl through batter.

8. Sprinkle sea salt evenly over the surface.

9. Bake 30 to 35 minutes, or until toothpick inserted in the middle comes out clean.

10. Let cool in pan before cutting.

FOR FURRY FRIENDS

● BONE UP DOG BISCUITS ●

All the dogs you know will be begging for these
bone-shaped biscuits.

....
MAKES 3 DOZEN TREATS
....

½ cup water

½ cup olive oil

2 eggs

2 cups flour

½ cup cornmeal

½ cup rolled oats

4 tablespoons peanut butter

1. Preheat oven to 400°F. Line baking sheet with parchment paper.

2. In a small bowl, beat water, oil and eggs together.

3. In a medium bowl, stir flour, cornmeal and oats, then fold in wet mixture.

4. Mix in peanut butter using rubber spatula until dough forms ball.

5. Roll out dough onto lightly floured surface, then use bone-shaped cookie cutter to cut out shapes.

6. Lay shapes on prepared baking sheet and bake 20 minutes. Turn off oven and allow biscuits to cool in oven until crisp.

7. Store in airtight container for 1 week.

FOR FURRY FRIENDS

● STARFISH CAT TREATS ●

Your feline friends will go into a frenzy for these fishy treats.

MAKES 3 DOZEN TREATS

1 ½ cup whole wheat flour

1 5 oz. can of
water-packed tuna, drained

1 large egg

1 tablespoon olive oil

2 teaspoons dried catnip

1. Preheat oven to 350°F. Line baking sheet with parchment paper and set aside.

2. Add flour, tuna, egg, olive oil and catnip to food processor bowl and blend until smooth.

3. Flatten dough on clean surface and cut shapes using mini star-shaped cookie cutters. Place stars on baking sheet.

4. Bake for 10 minutes or until treats are slightly brown. Let cool completely before feeding to your cat.

5. Store treats in an airtight container in the refrigerator for 1 week.

All styling by Jessica D'Argenio Waller
All other clothing not listed: models' own
All photography by Lindsay Hite

INTERNS
Alyson Katz, Laurise McMillian, Samantha Wilson

COVER CREDITS
Hair by Andrea Mitchell
Makeup by Ngozi Olandu

Clothing provided by:
Ban.do
Lulus.com
Wanderlust + Co.
XOXO

CHAPTER 2: ANYTIME PARTIES
SECRET GARDEN TEA PARTY
Hair by Roxanne Farias Walsh
Makeup by Stacy Leigh of Charm City Makeup
Prop styling by Krystal Jean Masson
of Esther & Harper

Clothing provided by:
Delia's
Jack BB Dakota
Juliet & Company
Lenora Dame
Lulus.com
Shop Lately
Urbanog.com

SUMMER SPA PARTY
Hair by Roxanne Farias Walsh
Makeup by Stacy Leigh of Charm City Makeup

STAR STYLE SWAP
Hair by Roxanne Farias Walsh
Makeup by Leah Bassett

Clothing provided by:
BOBS by Skechers
Lulus.com
Pink & Pepper
Shop Prima Donna
Silver Jeans Co.
SO
Steve Madden

POM POM PARTY
Hair by Andrea Mitchell
Makeup by Ngozi Olandu

Clothing provided by:
Ban.do
Betsey Johnson
G by Guess
Jessica Simpson
Keds
Lulus.com
Max & Chloe
Princess Vera Wang
Rampage
Ruby Rox
Shop Prima Donna
Wanderlust + Co.

COOKIE BAKE-OFF
Hair by Luis Bujia
Makeup by Leah Bassett

Clothing provided by:
Ali & Kris
Betsey Johnson
District Clothing
I Heart Ronson
Kitsch
Lulus.com
P.S. from Aeropostale
Urbanog.com
Wanderlust + Co.

CHAPTER 3: BIRTHDAY PARTIES
ICE CREAM SOCIAL
Hair by Roxanne Farias Walsh
Makeup by Leah Bassett

Clothing provided by:
2 Lips Too
Garnet Hill
Keds
Lulus.com
Others Follow
Shop Prima Donna

PET BIRTHDAY PARTY
Hair by Roxanne Farias Walsh
Makeup by Stacy Leigh of Charm City Makeup
Styled by Jessica D'Argenio Waller

Clothing provided by:
Levi's
Lulus.com

CREDITS

GLAMPING SLEEPOVER
Hair by Roxanne Farias Walsh
Makeup by Stacy Leigh of Charm City Makeup
Prop styling by Krystal Jean Masson
of Esther & Harper

Clothing provided by:
Ali & Kris
Bellatrix
Betsey Johnson
K. Bell
Lulus.com
Obey Propaganda
O'Neill
PACT Apparel
Rampage
Skechers
Urbanog.com
Vintage Havana
We Love Colors

MOVIE NIGHT SLUMBER PARTY
Hair by Luis Bujia
Makeup by Leah Bassett

Clothing provided by:
District Clothing
Hard Tail
Henry Mills
Jessica Simpson
Joe Fresh
Junk Food Clothing
K. Bell
Lily White
Lulus.com
O'Neill
P.S. from Aeropostale
SO
Under Armour

SPRINKLE SOIRÉE
Hair by Andrea Mitchell
Makeup by Ngozi Olandu

Clothing provided by:
Jessica Simpson
Kate Spade for Keds
Lulus.com
Macy's
Max & Chloe
Unique Vintage
Wanderlust + Co.

CHAPTER 4: HOLIDAY PARTIES
NEW YEAR'S FÊTE
Hair by Roxanne Farias Walsh
Makeup by Leah Bassett

Clothing provided by:
BOBS by Skechers
ILY Couture
Lulus.com
Princess Vera Wang
Prom Girl
Shop Prima Donna
Urbanog.com
XOXO

EASTER EGG PICNIC
Hair by Roxanne Farias Walsh
Makeup by Stacy Leigh
of Charm City Makeup

Clothing provided by:
Bellatrix
Levi's
Lulus.com

CHRISTMAS CARDI PARTY
Hair by Luis Bujia
Makeup by Leah Bassett

Clothing provided by:
Ban.do
Boohoo.com
Betsey Johnson
Elle
F89 by Fantas-Eyes
I Heart Ronson
Jack BB Dakota
Lulus.com
Marlyn Schiff
Others Follow
Roxy
Unique Vintage
XOXO